PRENTICE HALL
WRITING AND GRAMMAR

Reading Support Practice Book

Grade Eleven

PEARSON

Prentice Hall

Boston, Massachusetts,
Upper Saddle River, New Jersey

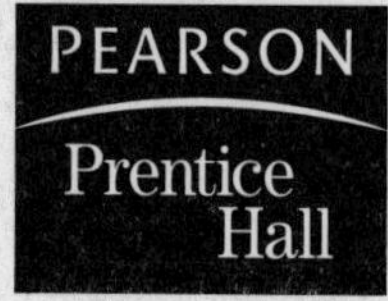

ISBN 0-13-361702-5

1 2 3 4 5 6 7 8 9 10   10 09 08 07 06

CONTENTS

PRETEST 1

VOCABULARY STRATEGIES

Context Clues
Guided Practice Worksheet **15**

Connotation/Denotation
Guided Practice Worksheet **19**

Multiple-Meaning Words
Guided Practice Worksheet **21**

COMPREHENSION STRATEGIES

**Active Reading: Preview
and Activate Prior Knowledge**
Guided Practice Worksheet **23**

Active Reading: Set a Purpose
Guided Practice Worksheet **25**

**Active Reading: Question
and Clarify**
Guided Practice Worksheet **27**

Active Reading: Connect
Guided Practice Worksheet **29**

Active Reading: KWL
Guided Practice Worksheet **31**

**Identify Main Idea and
Supporting Details**
Guided Practice Worksheet **33**

Make Inferences
Guided Practice Worksheet **37**

Compare and Contrast
Guided Practice Worksheet **39**

**Identify Steps in a Process or
Follow a Sequence of Events**
Guided Practice Worksheet **41**

Recognize Spatial Relationships
Guided Practice Worksheet **43**

Recognize Cause and Effect
Guided Practice Worksheet **45**

Identify Problems and Solutions
Guided Practice Worksheet **47**

Use Visual and Graphic Clues
Guided Practice Worksheet **49**

Interpret Figurative Language
Guided Practice Worksheet **51**

CRITICAL READING STRATEGIES

**Distinguish Between Important
and Unimportant Information**
Guided Practice Worksheet **53**

**Distinguish Between Fact and
Opinion or Nonfact**
Guided Practice Worksheet **55**

**Evaluate Author's Purpose and
Point of View**
Guided Practice Worksheet **59**

**Evaluate Evidence and
Sources of Information**
Guided Practice Worksheet **61**

Evaluate Author's Bias
Guided Practice Worksheet **63**

APPLICATION STRATEGIES

Draw Conclusions
Guided Practice Worksheet **65**

Summarize
Guided Practice Worksheet **67**

Paraphrase
Guided Practice Worksheet **69**

Form Generalizations
Guided Practice Worksheet **71**

Make Judgments
Guided Practice Worksheet **73**

Read the following passage. Then answer the questions that follow. Write the letter of the correct answer on the line at the right.

> The hair on her head was dark brown streaked with gray. Her old fur hat was gray, and it clung to the back of her neck—a squirrel with its furry back bent almost double in an effort to hold on. Her blue raincoat hung nearly to the ground in front and was several inches shorter in the back. She carried a shopping bag in each hand. In that city neighborhood, she was a sign of spring. Like a battered crocus or a soot-sprinkled daffodil planted too near the sidewalk, she shrugged off the dirt and burst forth each year. But she was a thorny flower. And none ventured too near, for she mumbled as she trudged from trash basket to trash basket, and anybody—child or adult—who got too close was liable to be jabbed with words that stung like sharp, prickly spines.

1. Why does the author say that the woman's hat is a squirrel?
   A. The hat is made of squirrel's fur.
   B. The hat's color and material resemble a squirrel.
   C. Squirrels climb on the woman and cling to her neck.
   D. The woman lives with the squirrels in the city neighborhood.

    1. ______

2. What does the woman do if she is approached by anyone?
   A. She jabs people, probably with an umbrella or walking cane.
   B. She pricks them with the thorny flowers she carries.
   C. She speaks harshly to them, using words that might hurt their feelings.
   D. She asks them to help her search for treasures in the trash baskets.

    2. ______

3. Using the context clues offered in the last sentence of the excerpt, explain what the author means by "none *ventured* too near . . ."
   A. No one risks getting too close to the woman.
   B. Getting near the woman is an adventure.
   C. Everyone watches the woman from a safe distance.
   D. People make bets on what the woman will do if someone gets close to her.

    3. ______

4. Using the information presented about the woman, what do you infer about the woman's social status?
   A. She is a person who lives on the streets and collects items from trash baskets.
   B. She is an irritable woman who has inadvertently thrown something away.
   C. She is an antisocial person who likes squirrels and flowers.
   D. She is a woman who derives joy from shopping but not socializing.

    4. ______

5. Based on the words the author uses to describe the woman, evaluate the author's opinion of the woman.
   A. Since the author calls her "a sign of spring" and compares her to a flower, the author thinks she is beautiful in her own way.
   B. The author does not like her because she uses unkind words toward people who approach her.
   C. The author is prejudiced against her because she looks shabby, searches through trash baskets, and frightens people away.
   D. Since the author emphasizes the woman's charm behind the ragged clothes and cantankerous attitude, the writer's opinion of the woman is positive.

    5. ______

6. What do you presume the author's response would be if the woman was   6. _______
   banished from the neighborhood?
   A. The author would support the exile because the woman's appearance
      disgraces the neighborhood.
   B. The author would miss the woman because her annual reappearance
      reminds the author of spring and flowers.
   C. The author would feel relief for the children and adults who feared the woman.
   D. The author would be glad to know that no one would be rifling through his
      trash any longer.

Read the following passage. Then answer the questions that follow. Write the letter
of the correct answer on the line at the right.

> As we were thus conversing in a low tone while Old Barley's sustained growl
> vibrated in the beam that crossed the ceiling, the room door opened, and a very
> pretty, slight, dark-eyed girl of twenty or so came in with a basket in her hand:
> whom Herbert tenderly relieved of the basket, and presented blushing as "Clara."
> She really was a most charming girl, and might have passed for a captive fairy
> whom the truculent ogre, Old Barley, had pressed into his service.

7. Which of the following statements is a fact presented in the selection?   7. _______
   A. Clara has dark eyes and a slight build.
   B. Clara is charming and resembles a captive fairy.
   C. The narrator can barely hear Old Barley's faint, whispering voice.
   D. Clara's looks resemble those of her father.

8. Which of the following statements is an opinion presented in the selection?   8. _______
   A. The girl is in her early twenties.
   B. A girl named Clara entered the room carrying a basket.
   C. Clara is a charming girl.
   D. The narrator is conversing with a man named Herbert.

Read the following passage. Then answer the questions that follow. Write the letter
of the correct answer on the line at the right.

> With a smother of foam and bubbles the green water closed over me. When I
> was not too far down, I signaled the crew above to stop. Since they were new at
> this business, I wanted to see whether they would answer satisfactorily. When
> they promptly did so, I adjusted the air pressure in my diving dress and resumed
> my slow descent.

9. In which sentence in the excerpt can you find the paragraph's main idea?   9. _______
   A. Sentence one   B. Sentence two   C. Sentence three   D. Sentence four

10. How does the diver test the crew's ability to answer satisfactorily?   10. _______
    A. The diver adjusts the air pressure and descends slowly.
    B. Before descending very far, the diver signals the crew to stop.
    C. The diver stops just beneath the water and waits for the crew's reaction.
    D. The diver stops several times to determine if the crew is paying attention.

Read the following passage. Then answer the questions that follow. Write the letter of the correct answer on the line at the right.

> The record book will tell you that Roberto Clemente collected 3,000 hits during his major-league career. It will say that he came to bat 9,454 times, that he drove in 1,305 runs, and played 2,433 games over an eighteen-year span.
>
> But it won't tell you about Carolina, Puerto Rico, and the old square, and the narrow, twisting streets, and the roots that produced him. It won't tell you about the Julio Coronado School and a remarkable woman named Maria Isabella Casares, whom he called "Teacher" until the day he died and who helped to shape his life in times of despair and depression . . . .
>
> And most of all, those cold numbers won't begin to delineate the man Roberto Clemente was. To even begin to understand what this magnificent athlete was all about, you have to work backward. The search begins at the site of its ending.

11. What is the author's purpose in writing about Roberto Clemente?   11. ______
    A. The author wants to share Clemente's impressive baseball statistics.
    B. The author wants readers to know where Clemente was born.
    C. The author wants to write about famous baseball players from Puerto Rico.
    D. The author wants to reveal the man Clemente was by talking about the important people and places in his life.

12. Which of the following best describes the author's point of view toward   12. ______
    Roberto Clemente?
    A. The author is impressed with Clemente's baseball records.
    B. The author is prejudiced against Clemente because he was from Puerto Rico.
    C. The author greatly admires Clemente, and he wants to give credit to the people and places that molded Clemente into a great baseball player.
    D. The author believes that baseball records should include background infor-mation about the players.

13. Choose the meaning that best fits the way *delineate* is used in the third   13. ______
    paragraph of the excerpt.
    A. to trace the outline of; sketch out
    B. to draw
    C. to depict in words; describe
    D. make colorful

Use this chart to answer the following questions.

Name of Spacecraft	Dates Launched and Recovered	Maximum Distance from Earth	Duration of Flight
Freedom 7	May 5, 1961	116 miles	15 minutes
Apollo 8	December 21–27, 1968	231,000 miles	146 hours, 59 minutes, 49 seconds
Shuttle Challenger	June 18–24, 1983	187 miles	6 days, 2 hours, 24 minutes
Shuttle Discovery	August 30 to September 5, 1984	185 miles	6 days, 56 minutes

On the line at the right, write the letter of the correct answer.

14. Which spacecraft traveled the farthest distance from Earth?   14. ______
   A. *Freedom 7*   **C.** *Shuttle Challenger*
   B. *Apollo 8*   **D.** *Shuttle Discovery*

15. What was the duration of *Shuttle Challenger's* flight?   15. ______
   A. less than 147 hours   **C.** two weeks
   B. exactly six days   **D.** slightly more than six days

Read the following passage. Then answer the questions that follow. Write the letter of the correct answer on the line at the right.

Emily walked to the desk which sat directly under a sign with the neatly printed words "Motorcoach Tours." She waited for the man sitting at the desk to look up. He smiled and asked, "May I help you?" Emily shyly gestured toward the sign.

"Excuse me," she began, "but what is a 'Motorcoach Tour'?" The man's eyebrows lifted.

"Well," he said, "it's a <u>bus</u> tour!"

Emily thought about his answer for a moment.

"Then," she murmured, "—can I ask a question? Why doesn't the sign say 'Bus Tours'?"

"Easy. More people like <u>motorcoach</u> tours."

"Are they different from bus tours?"

"Nope. We use the same buses," the man declared, "but people just won't buy tickets for <u>bus</u> tours the way they'll buy tickets for <u>motorcoach</u> tours!"

16. What generalization can you make about people who buy motorcoach tour tickets? 16. ______
   A. They prefer the term *motorcoach* to *bus*.
   B. They buy more tickets when the sign at the ticket office displays neatly printed words.
   C. They are curious about the company's use of the word *motorcoach* instead of the word *bus*.
   D. They prefer to buy tickets from friendly ticket salespersons.

17. The people who buy tickets for the Motorcoach Tours are making the   17. ______
connotation that
    A. they are riding in a luxury vehicle used only by the elite.
    B. they are riding in an antique vehicle.
    C. they are taking a bus.
    D. they are special people.

18. If the people who buy motorcoach tickets consider the denotation of the term   18. ______
motorcoach, they will realize, like Emily, that it means what?
    A. a luxury vehicle used only by the elite
    B. a powerful automobile equipped with mighty engines and piloted by well-
       trained personnel
    C. an antique horse-drawn carriage that has been outfitted with a motor
    D. a bus

Read the following passage. Then answer the questions that follow. Write the letter
of the correct answer on the line at the right.

> **Watson.** But, Holmes—if she's correct in saying the door and window of her
> sister's room were locked, then the girl must have been absolutely alone when
> she met her death.
>
> **Holmes.** Death in a sealed room, in fact?
>
> **Watson.** Natural causes. No other explanation. [Scratching his head.] But then,
> what about that whistling in the night—and that speckled band business?
>
> **Holmes.** I was hoping **you** were going to provide me with those answers, my
> dear Watson.
>
> **Watson.** Well, you'll have to hope again!
>
> **Holmes.** [Mock dismay.] Dear me!
>
> **Watson.** Have you any ideas?
>
> **Holmes.** We have whistles at night, a band of gypsies . . .
>
> **Watson.** Yes.
>
> **Holmes.** . . . a doctor who has a financial interest in preventing his step-
> daughter's marriage.
>
> **Watson.** Ah, yes!
>
> **Holmes.** And we have a dying reference to a speckled band. Now, if we combine
> all these elements, I think there is good ground to believe that the mystery may
> be cleared up.

19. How are the thought processes of Watson and Holmes different?   19. ______
    A. They view death in a locked room diversely.
    B. They do not feel the same sense of curiosity about the speckled band.
    C. They do not agree that the stepfather's financial interest is important to
       solving the case.
    D. They have different opinions about the cause of the whistling in the night.

20. All but one of the following comparisons of Watson and Holmes is true. Locate   **20.** ______
the one comparison that is false.
  A. They are very slow to draw conclusions about the death in the locked room.
  B. They listen to each other's opinions.
  C. They do not ridicule each other's reasoning.
  D. They both have an appetite for solving mysteries.

21. Which of the following statements best summarizes the passage?   **21.** ______
  A. Watson thinks the sister died of natural causes.
  B. Holmes believes the stepfather's financial interest is the key to solving
    the mystery.
  C. Watson and Holmes consider and combine all the clues related to the
    sister's death.
  D. Watson and Holmes are curious men who cannot resist a good mystery.

22. What conclusion about the sister's death can be drawn based on Holmes and   **22.** ______
Watson's conversation?
  A. She died of natural causes.
  B. She was murdered.
  C. Her death is definitely related to a group of gypsies, a whistle in the night,
    and a speckled band.
  D. The remaining sister knows the truth about her sister's death.

23. Which of the following pieces of evidence do you think is most influential   **23.** ______
in leading Holmes to discount Watson's suggestion that the sister died of
natural causes?
  A. The window and door of the sister's room were locked.
  B. The sister made a dying reference to a speckled band.
  C. The stepfather has a financial interest in preventing his stepdaughter's marriage.
  D. A band of gypsies is mentioned.

24. Which reference source would give you information about Sir Arthur Conan   **24.** ______
Doyle, the author of the Sherlock Holmes stories?
  A. almanac
  B. *Readers' Guide to Periodical Literature*
  C. dictionary
  D. encyclopedia

Read the following passage. Then answer the questions that follow. Write the letter
of the correct answer on the line at the right.

The form of a poem is its overall pattern. You can get a sense of form simply by
looking at a poem on the page. The poem may be broken into even parts, like
bread cut into slices, or it may be presented uninterrupted, as a whole, uncut loaf.
The lines of the poem may be similar in length, creating a visual pattern on the
paper. Words may even be arranged to form a picture. A poet can construct a poem
by using a known pattern or by making one up. In either case the finished
creation will have a shape and form.

25. Which statement best expresses the implied main idea of the passage?   25. ______
    A. Poets can give their poems shape and form by a variety of techniques.
    B. Some poems are broken into even parts, and some are presented uninterrupted.
    C. Poets like to make their own decisions about the visual quality of their poems.
    D. The words of a poem form a visual shape on the paper.

26. What appeal does poetry have for the writer who enjoys freedom of expression?   26. ______
    A. Poetry can be written using any pattern the poet chooses, even innovative
       patterns.
    B. Poetry can be made to resemble a loaf of bread.
    C. Poetry's visual appeal is just as important as its content.
    D. Poetry's form is a result of its overall pattern.

Read the following passage. Then answer the questions that follow. Write the letter
of the correct answer on the line at the right.

> At breakfast on our chosen day, when Mama, Daddy, and Aunt Nicey were in
> the dining room, I brought Doodle to the door in the go-cart just as usual and
> had them turn their backs, making them cross their hearts and hope to die if they
> peeked. I helped Doodle up, and when he was standing alone I let them look.
> There wasn't a sound as Doodle walked slowly across the room and sat down at
> his place at the table. Then Mama began to cry and ran over to him, hugging
> him and kissing him. Daddy hugged him, too, so I went to Aunt Nicey who was
> thanks praying in the doorway, and began to waltz her around. We danced
> together quite well until she came down on my big toe with her brogans, hurting
> me so badly I thought I was crippled for life.

27. What did the narrator do just before helping Doodle to stand up?   27. ______
    A. He ate breakfast.
    B. He asked his family to promise not to peek.
    C. He instructed his family to walk slowly out of the room.
    D. He gave Doodle an encouraging wink.

28. Which of the following can be concluded from this passage?   28. ______
    A. Doodle had finally recovered from his injury.
    B. Aunt Nicey resented her dependence on Doodle's parents.
    C. Doodle's family was proud of his surprising new accomplishment.
    D. Go-carts were frequently substituted for wheelchairs.

29. Which of the following statements best expresses the problem Doodle had   29. ______
    before his surprise walk across the dining room?
    A. Doodle was spoiled by the go-cart and demanded that he be pulled around
       the house.
    B. Doodle suffered from an unidentified disorder that interfered with his
       ability to walk.
    C. Aunt Nicey stepped on Doodle's big toe, crippling him for life.
    D. Doodle is a toddler who is taking his first steps.

NAME _________________________________   DATE _____________

30. Which is the best hypothesis to explain how Doodle's problem was solved?   30. ______
    A. Aunt Nicey assisted Doodle in his goal to learn to walk.
    B. A physical therapist taught Doodle to walk, and the narrator was the first
       member of the family to witness the results.
    C. Mama and Daddy put Doodle in a hospital where he learned to walk.
    D. The narrator worked with Doodle for a period of time to help him walk.

Read the following passage. Then answer the questions that follow. Write the letter
of the correct answer on the line at the right.

> . . . The occupants of the carriage were a small girl, and a smaller girl, and a small
> boy. An aunt belonging to the children occupied one corner seat, and the further
> corner seat on the opposite side was occupied by a bachelor, who was a stranger
> to their party, but the small girls and the small boy emphatically occupied the
> compartment . . . .
>
>   "Don't, Cyril, don't," exclaimed the aunt, as the small boy began smacking
> the cushions of the seat, producing a cloud of dust at each blow.

31. How can the aunt's seat best be described in relationship to the bachelor's seat?   31. ______
    A. The aunt occupies the same side of the carriage as the bachelor.
    B. The aunt sits between two of the children, the third child sitting next to the
       bachelor.
    C. The aunt sits directly across from the bachelor.
    D. The aunt sits diagonally across from the bachelor.

32. According to the selection, what causes the aunt to admonish Cyril?   32. ______
    A. Cyril occupies more than his share of a carriage seat.
    B. Cyril smacks the seat cushions, causing clouds of dust to erupt.
    C. Cyril annoys the bachelor by continually moving about the carriage's interior.
    D. The aunt enjoys criticizing the children's behavior.

33. Choose the meaning that best fits the way the term *emphatically* is used in   33. ______
    the passage.
    A. in a way that is expressed, felt, or done with emphasis
    B. in a way that uses emphasis in speaking, expressing, etc.
    C. in a way that attracts attention; very noticeable; striking

Read the following passage. Then answer the questions that follow. Write the letter of the correct answer on the line at the right.

> While we packed the breakfast dishes, Papa went outside to start the "Carcanchita." That was the name Papa gave his old '38 black Plymouth. He bought it in a used-car lot in Santa Rosa in the winter of 1949. Papa was very proud of his car. "Mi Carcanchita," my little jalopy, he called it. He had a right to be proud of it. He spent a lot of time looking at other cars before buying this one. When he finally chose the "Carcanchita," he checked it thoroughly before driving it out of the car lot. He examined every inch of the car. He listened to the motor, tilting his head from side to side like a parrot, trying to detect any noises that spelled car trouble. After being satisfied with the looks and sounds of the car, Papa insisted on knowing who the original owner was. He never did find out from the car salesman. But he bought the car anyway. Papa figured the original owner must have been an important man because behind the rear seat of the car he found a blue necktie.

34. Some information in the selection is important and some is unimportant. Choose the statement below that is not important to the main idea of this passage.   **34.** _______
   A. Papa named his car "Carcanchita."
   B. Papa examined every inch of the car before buying it.
   C. The tie Papa found in the rear seat of the car was blue.
   D. Papa looked at other cars before buying the '38 Plymouth.

35. What type of context clues does the author give the reader about the meaning of the description "a blue necktie"?   **35.** _______
   A. Papa never wore a blue necktie.
   B. Only someone who could wear a necktie would buy a good car.
   C. The author thinks blue neckties are tasteful.
   D. Papa will always keep the necktie.

Read the following sentence and answer the question that follows. Write the letter of the correct answer on the line at the right.

> The moon swung high over us and there was no sleeping for brightness.

36. Which of the following sentences best paraphrases the sentence above?   **36.** _______
   A. The moon swung high over us and there was no sleeping for the brightness.
   B. The moon hung high in the sky and we could not sleep because it was so bright.
   C. We slept well because the moon was so high in the sky.
   D. We were able to sleep because it was so dark.

NAME ____ DATE _______________

Read the following passage. Then answer the question that follows. Write the letter of the correct answer on the line at the right.

> Perhaps if Laura knew how difficult a task she faced, her spirits would have failed. But she delighted in each new discovery, no matter how small. Every new word was a new adventure. Bit by bit she added to her knowledge.
>
> She learned that the shapes were letters of the alphabet and that the letters made words.
>
> When Laura seemed to have a firm idea of the use of letters, Dr. Howe called in another teacher to instruct Laura in the manual alphabet. This system, developed for the deaf, employs a different finger position for each letter. Laura would place her hand over her teacher's and feel the positions for each letter. By January, just three months after coming to the institution, Laura had mastered the manual alphabet.

37. Which sentence(s) in this excerpt gives the main idea?   37. ______
    A. The last sentence   C. The fourth sentence
    B. The second and third sentences   D. The fifth sentence

Read the following passage. Then answer the question that follows. Write the letter of the correct answer on the line at the right.

> Being thirteen has certain problems that only another thirteen-year-old would understand. The biggest, I think, is learning how to get along with adults. I have found that when dealing with grown-ups, it is wise to remember two things:
>   1. Always use your head.
>   2. Never use your head.

38. Based on the above information, what do you infer about what a thirteen-year-   38. ______
    old should remember?
    A. Sometimes things don't make sense.
    B. Only another thirteen-year-old can understand adults.
    C. Getting along with adults is a problem.
    D. Don't worry about anything.

Read the passage below. Then answer the question that follows by writing the letter of the correct answer on the line at the right.

> "One of the best ways is to use a honey box, " I replied. "You fill a small open box with honey and set it outside. Worker bees will gorge on honey and carry it to their hive. You sight their direction of flight against a distant tree or rock. That's a 'beeline.' You gradually work your way along the beeline, moving the honey box as you go. Eventually the workers will lead you right to their hive."

39. Why can a honey box lead you to a beehive?   39. ______
    A. You carry the box with you whenever you go.
    B. Worker bees will eat the honey.
    C. Worker bees will gorge on the honey and carry it to their hive.
    D. You find the "beeline" and then give the bees honey.

NAME ____ **DATE** _______________

Read the following passage. Then answer the question that follows by writing the letter of the correct answer on the line at the right.

> At last, twisting abruptly between two river islands, he came upon the mighty Yukon sweeping grandly to the north. He could not see from bank to bank, and in the quick-falling twilight it loomed a great white sea of frozen stillness.

40. How can the location of the Yukon best be described from the description above?   **40.** _______
   A. from side to side by two islands
   B. between two islands to the south
   C. he could not from the bank
   D. between two islands to the north

Read the passage below. Then answer the question that follows by writing the letter of the correct answer on the line at the right.

> The Whittington family was one of those hardest hit. The father had been killed in France and the grieving mother died soon afterward. Their young son, Dick, was left alone in the world. The boy was too young to take care of the farm which had supported them and soon it was nothing but overgrown weeds. The cattle were seized by the soldiers and the farms were falling down. Dick could find no work in the village and even if he had not been too proud to accept charity, there was no one to whom he could turn. He made up his mind to try to find work in the city and started out for London.

41. Why did Dick choose to leave the family farm?   **41.** _______
   A. His parents were poor.
   B. All the cattle died.
   C. Dick was curious about London.
   D. He had no family, was too young to take care of the farm, and needed to find work.

NAME _______________________________   DATE _______

Read the following passage. Then answer the questions that follow. Write the letter of the correct answer on the line at the right.

Walt Masters is not a very large boy, but there is manliness in his make-up, and he himself, although he does not know a great deal that most boys know, knows much that other boys do not know. He has never seen a train of cars nor an elevator in his life, and for that matter he has never once looked upon a cornfield, a plow, a cow, or even a chicken. He has never had a pair of shoes on his feet, nor gone to a picnic or a party, nor talked to a girl. But he has seen the sun at midnight, watched the ice jams on one of the mightiest rivers, and played beneath the northern lights, the one white child in thousands of square miles of frozen wilderness.

Walt has walked all the fourteen years of his life in suntanned, Moose-hide moccasins, and he can go to the Indian camps and "talk big" with the men, and trade *calico* beads with them for their precious furs. He can make bread without baking powder, yeast, or hops, shoot a moose at three hundred yards, and drive the wild wolf dogs fifty miles a day on the packed trail.

Last of all, he has a good heart, and is not afraid of the darkness and loneliness, of man or beast or thing. His father is a good man, strong and brave, and Walt is growing up like him.

42. Some information in the selection is important and some is not important.   42. ______
Choose the statement below that is *not* important to the main idea of
this passage.
   A. Walt has a good heart like his father.
   B. Walt knows how to "talk big" with the men.
   C. Walt can make bread without baking powder.
   D. Walt is fourteen.

43. Which of the following statements best summarize this passage?   43. ______
   A. Walt is very mature and wise for his age.
   B. Walt is a survivor in the wilderness.
   C. Walt is uncivilized.
   D. Walt is independent, good hearted, and dignified.

44. Which of the following sentences is a paraphrase for the first sentence of   44. ______
the selection?
   A. Walt Masters is not a very large boy, but there is manliness in his make-up,
      and he himself, although he does not know a great deal that most boys
      know, knows much that others boys do not know.
   B. Walt Masters is smarter than he looks.
   C. Walt Masters is not a big person but he has a masculine way about him,
      and knows things most boys don't know and doesn't know things most
      boys do know.
   D. Walt Masters is not that significant and is not popular with other boys.

45. What generalization can you make about people who live in the wilderness?   45. ______
   A. They hate to wear clothes.
   B. They are slow thinkers.
   C. They have no fun—they only hunt and try to survive in the harsh wilderness.
   D. They are resourceful, do not act carelessly, and love nature.

46. Based upon your reading this passage, what kind of judgment can you make   46. ______
about Walt?
   A. Walt likes to wear only animal furs and moccasins.
   B. Walt misses his mother.
   C. Walt likes people but is not afraid to be alone.
   D. Since Walt lives in the wilderness, he hasn't any manners.

NAME ___________________________________ DATE ___________

CONTEXT CLUES

Introduction

When you come across an unfamiliar word while reading, look for
context clues to help you figure out its meaning. **Context clues** are the
guides or keys in the words, phrases, and sentences that surround the
unknown word.

Types of Context Clues
- synonyms
- comparisons
- explanations
- definitions
- clues that provide a general sense of the word

Model 1

As you read this sentence from "Leiningen Versus the Ants," by Carl
Stephenson, notice how the underlined context clues give the reader a
general sense of the meaning of the word *reckon*.

> Leiningen . . . withdrew to his office, and began to **reckon** up his losses.
> He <u>estimated</u> these as large, but in comparison with his <u>bank balance</u>, by
> no means unbearable.

A careful reader would most likely guess that the word *reckon* has
something to do with keeping track of finances. The reader might then
define *reckon* as follows: *to make a calculation.*

Model 2

As you read this passage, look for a synonym of the word *weir.*

> It was possible—yes, if one could only get to the dam! A distance of nearly
> two miles lay between the ranch house and the **weir**—two miles of ants.

Were you able to guess the meaning of the word? A *weir* is a dam placed
across a river or canal to raise or divert water.

Model 3

In this passage, notice how a comparison helps define the word *hypnotize.*

> Perhaps the ants weren't so almighty, after all; perhaps he had allowed
> the mass suggestion of that evil black throng to **hypnotize** him, <u>just as</u>
> <u>a snake fascinates and overpowers</u>.

How would you define *hypnotize* based on this comparison?

   Context Clues   **15**

NAME _______________________ DATE _______________

Practice

Part I

The passages that follow are also from "Leiningen Versus the Ants," by
Carl Stephenson. On the lines provided, write context clues that help
you define the underlined words. Then write a definition of each word.
Check your definition in the dictionary.

> The ranch house and outbuildings stood upon rising ground. Their foun-
> dations were higher than the <u>breakwater</u>, so the flood would not reach them.

1. Unknown word: breakwater

Context Clues:

____

____

____

____

____

Definition:

____

____

____

> Leiningen got up on a chair. "Hey, lads, listen to me!" he cried. Slowly
> and <u>listlessly</u>, from all sides of the trench, the men began to shuffle toward
> him, the apathy of death already stamped on their faces.

2. Unknown word: listlessly

Context Clues:

____

____

____

____

Definition:

____

____

____

Part II

The following passage is from "The Bit of String," by Guy de Maupassant. Read the passage. Then complete the chart on the next page.

Master Hauchecorne of Bréauté had just arrived at Goderville, and was going toward the square when he saw on the ground a bit of string. Master Hauchecorne, <u>economist</u>, like every true Norman, thought that anything might be of use worth picking up, and he bent down painfully, for he suffered from rheumatism. He took up the piece of string, and was winding it carefully, when he noticed Malandin, the harness-maker, watching him from his doorway. The two men had long ago had a quarrel about a halter, and both being <u>vindictive</u>, had remained unfriendly. Hauchecorne was seized with a kind of shame, at thus being seen by his enemy picking a bit of twine out of the mud. He quickly hid his prize under his blouse, then in his breeches pocket; then he pretended to search the ground again for something which he did not find, and he went off toward the market, his head in advance, bent double by his <u>infirmities</u>.

He was forthwith lost in the noisy, shuffling crowd everywhere in motion from innumerable buyings and sellings . . . . The women, putting their great baskets down at their feet, had drawn out their fowls, which were lying on the ground, legs bound, eyes wild, combs scarlet. They listened to offers, held to their prices unmoved, their faces inscrutable; or suddenly deciding to accept an offer, cried out to the would-be purchaser slowly moving away:

"Agreed Master Hutine; I will give it at your price."

Then little by little the square emptied, and the Angelus sounding noon, those who lived too far to go home <u>dispersed</u> in the various public houses.

NAME ________________________ DATE __________

Unfamiliar Word	Context Clues	Definition
economist		
vindictive		
infirmities		
dispersed		

CONNOTATION/DENOTATION

Introduction

Every word has an exact, specific meaning, or **denotation.** A word's denotation is its dictionary definition. The denotative meaning of a word does not necessarily have positive or negative feelings associated with it.

Sometimes a word also has a **connotation,** a shade of meaning that comes from attitudes or emotional meaning connected to the word. A word's connotation is usually either positive or negative. Two words can have similar denotations, but their connotations can differ.

Notice the difference in meaning between the words in italics in the following sentences:

Examples

Among his troops, Gregorio is known as a fearless *leader.*

Among his troops, Gregorio is known as a fearless *dictator.*

The denotations, or dictionary meanings, of *leader* and *dictator* are similar. However, in the first sentence, leader has a positive connotation, while the word dictator has a negative connotation because it refers to someone who leads or rules in a cruel way.

Read the following pairs of sentences. Note the differences in connotation between the words in italics.

Examples

By noon, a *group* had gathered on the Capitol steps.

By noon, a *mob* had gathered on the Capitol steps.

The denotations of *group* and *mob* both indicate a crowd of people. However, *mob is* usually used in a negative sense to indicate a disorderly or unruly crowd.

The sound of *loud* applause reached Walter's ears as he approached the finish line.

The sound of *thunderous* applause reached Walter's ears as he approached the finish line.

Loud and *thunderous* both denote an intensity of sound. However, *thunderous,* in this incident, has a positive connotation because it indicates that there is an excitement and electricity in the crowd's response to Walter as he approached the finish line.

Reading Tip

As you read, keep in mind that writers convey their judgments and feelings about a subject by the words they choose. Pay particular attention to the connotations of specific words. A writer who describes a character's action as *foolhardy,* instead of *courageous, is* inviting the reader to share an attitude.

NAME _______________________________________ **DATE** _____________

Practice

Read the following passage from "The White Umbrella" by Gish Jen.

> The umbrella glowed like a scepter on the blue carpet while Mona, slumping over the keyboard, managed to eke out a fair rendition of a catfight. At the end of the piece, Miss Crosman asked her to stand up.
>
> "Stay right there," she said, then came back a minute later with a towel to cover the bench. "You must be cold," she continued. "Shall I call your mother and have her bring over some dry clothes?"
>
> "No," answered Mona. "She won't come because she . . . "
>
> "She's too busy," I broke in from the back of the room.
>
> "I see." Miss Crosman sighed and shook her head a little. "Your glasses are filthy, honey," she said to Mona. "Shall I clean them for you?"
>
> Sisterly embarrassment seized me. Why hadn't Mona wiped her lenses when I told her to? As she resumed abuse of the piano, I stared at the umbrella. I wanted to open it, twirl it around by its slender silver handle; I wanted to dangle it from my wrist on the way to school the way the other girls did. I wondered what Miss Crosman would say if I offered to bring it to Eugenie at school tomorrow. She would be impressed with my consideration for others; Eugenie would be pleased to have it back; and I would have possession of the umbrella for an entire night. I looked at it again, toying with the idea of asking for one for Christmas. I knew, however, how my mother would react.

A. Connotation/Denotation

In the dictionary find the denotation of each of these general words, and write it in the second column. Then find a word in the passage that has a similar meaning. Write the word in the third column. In the fourth column indicate whether the word from the passage has a positive or negative connotation.

General Word	Denotation	Related Word	Connotation
shone			
leaning			
dirty			
grabbed			
thin			

B. Challenge!

For each of these general words, write a word that has the same denotation. Label the new word positive or negative. Then, write sentences using your words. Your sentences should express the connotations of the words.

1. eat ____
2. cold ____
3. walk ____

MULTIPLE-MEANING WORDS

Introduction

Readers often encounter words with more than one meaning. To determine the sense in which such **multiple-meaning words** are used, it is necessary to look at the context in which they are used. A word's context is made up of the sentence in which it appears and/or the parts of the passage immediately surrounding it. By considering a multiple-meaning word's context, the reader can determine which meaning is appropriate.

Note the differences in the meaning of pupil in the following sentences.

The *pupil* stood beside her desk and began to recite the poem.

The *pupil* in each eye widened as the light grew dimmer.

In the first sentence, the meaning of *pupil* is "a young person in school; a student." In the second sentence, the meaning of *pupil* is "an opening through which light enters the eye." Context clues in each sentence help you to determine the meaning of *pupil* in each sentence.

Most dictionaries contain a numbered definition for each meaning of a word. For some words, such as *point*, there can be as many as twenty definitions.

Study the multiple-meaning words shown on the chart below. Note how the context clues in each of the example sentences reveal the meaning of the word as it is being used.

Word	Meaning	Example
vision	• a picture created by the imagination • sight	• Marta had a *vision* of how to illustrate her poster. • These glasses will improve your *vision*.
admit	• to allow to enter • to make known, usually unwillingly	• The theater manager planned to *admit* one hundred people to see the show. • We had to finally *admit* that the project was a failure.
company	• guests or visitors at one's home • a business	• My brothers and I cleaned the house before the *company* arrived. • Tran works at a *company* that manufactures athletic shoes.
operation	• a kind of surgery • the quality or state of being able to work	• Nanna's hip *operation* was successful. • The new factory is now in *operation*.

Practice

Read the following passage from "The No-Guitar Blues," by Gary Soto.

> He had watched "American Bandstand" for years and had heard Ray Camacho and the Teardrops at Romain Playground, but it had never occurred to him that he too might become a musician. That afternoon Fausto knew his mission in life: to play guitar in his own band; to sweat out his songs and prance around the stage; to make money and dress weird.
>
> Fausto turned off the television set and walked outside, wondering how he could get enough money to buy a guitar. He couldn't ask his parents because they would just say, "Money doesn't grow on trees" or "What do you think we are, bankers?" And besides, they hated rock music. They were into the conjunto music of Lydia Mendoza, Flaco Jimenez, and Little Joe and La Familia. And, as Fausto recalled, the last album they bought was *The Chipmunks Sing Christmas Favorites*.

A. Multiple-Meaning Words

Find five words in the passage that have more than one meaning. In the left column, write each word and its meaning as used in the passage. In the right column, write a sentence that illustrates a different meaning of the word.

Word/Meaning in the Passage	Sentence That Illustrates a Different Meaning

B. Challenge!

Write two sentences that demonstrate different meanings for *one* of the following words: *service, general, deposit, force.*

____

____

NAME ____ **DATE** __________

ACTIVE READING: PREVIEW AND ACTIVATE PRIOR KNOWLEDGE

Introduction

When you read, you very often use the knowledge you already have about a subject to understand and predict the outcome of a story. This is called **activating prior knowledge**.

Reading Tip
Activate prior knowledge by asking yourself the following questions:
1. Does the title of the piece give any clues to its contents?
2. What is the subject of the writing?
3. What do I already know about the subject?
4. Have I read about the subject before? What did I learn?

Read the following passage from "The Medicine Bag," by Virginia Driving Hawk Sneve. Refer to the reading tip and answer the questions posed there. For example, the title, the author's name, and the first sentence reveal that the passage relates to Native American culture. Do you already know or have you read anything about Native American cultures and traditions? Have you read pieces of Native American literature? Compare your own answers to the answers that follow the passage.

> My kid sister Cheryl and I always bragged about our Sioux grandpa, Joe Iron Shell. Our friends who had always lived in the city and only knew about Indians from movies and TV were impressed by our stories. Maybe we exaggerated and made Grandpa and the reservation sound glamorous, but when we'd return home to Iowa after our yearly summer visit to Grandpa, we always had some exciting tale to tell.
>
> We always had some authentic Sioux article to show our listeners. One year Cheryl had new moccasins that Grandpa had made. On another visit he gave me a small, round, flat, rawhide drum that was decorated with a painting of a warrior riding a horse. He taught me a real Sioux chant to sing while I beat the drum with a leather-covered stick that had a feather on the end . . . .

Sample: Activate Prior Knowledge
1. What I already know: There are many different Native American groups.
2. What I've read about this subject before: I have read a number of Native American folktales. I've also read about Native Americans in my history books. The books revealed that the Native Americans have a deep respect for nature.

NAME ____   DATE _______________

Practice

Below is another passage from "The Medicine Bag." Answer the questions that follow it.

> . . . We never showed our friends Grandpa's picture. Not that we were ashamed of him, but because we knew that the glamorous tales we told didn't go with the real thing. Our friends would have laughed at the picture because Grandpa wasn't tall and stately like TV Indians. His hair wasn't in braids but hung in stringy gray strands on his neck, and he was old. He was our great-grandfather, and he didn't live in a tipi but all by himself in a part log, part tar-paper shack on the Rosebud Reservation in South Dakota. So when Grandpa came to visit us, I was so ashamed and embarrassed I could've died.

1. Before you read the second passage and you heard the stories of Joe Iron Shell, how did you imagine him to be?

   ____

   ____

2. Does this image of the girls' grandfather come as a surprise? Had you predicted a more glamorous man? Were you perhaps activating prior knowledge by thinking of the Native Americans as they appeared in old TV movies?

   ____

   ____

3. Did the author surprise you by first mentioning the "glamorous tales" that the girls told, *then* showing you that grandpa was really very old and not particularly glamorous? Why do you think she did this?

   ____

   ____

ACTIVE READING: SET A PURPOSE

Introduction

Different types of writing present different reasons for reading. For example, we usually read textbooks to gather information and we read stories for pleasure. The first sentence or paragraph of a selection will usually indicate the kind of writing that follows. For example, when you read the passage below, you will probably know what kind of story will follow.

Asking Questions to Set a Purpose
Setting a purpose for reading involves identifying specific questions that you will answer during reading. By asking yourself questions before you begin, you direct your attention to the key ideas in the passage. You can get an idea of what the selection is about through looking at the title, illustrations, and subheadings. You may also want to read the first sentence or passage for further information.

Setting a Purpose: Three Steps
  1. Study title and illustrations of selection.
  2. Read the first sentence or paragraph.
  3. Look for clues in the text. (Is the writing informative or entertaining?)

Model

Read the following passage from the beginning of "Why Badger Is So Humble," by Mourning Dove. Think of your own questions that you could use to set a purpose for reading the entire section as a whole. Then compare your questions to the ones below.

> One time Why-ay'-looh-Fox and Coyote were living in the same lodge. The hunting was poor, and they became very hungry. They hunted hard every sun but did not find any game.

Questions
What kind of story is this?
  • A folk tale

Purpose for Reading
Why would someone choose to read this passage?
  • For enjoyment
  • To learn a lesson
  • Find out about other cultures and beliefs

NAME _______________________________________   **DATE** _____________

Practice

Below is a passage from "Hyacinth Drift," by Marjorie Kinnan Rawlings.
Read the passage and answer the questions that follow.

The St. John's River flows from south to north and empties into the
Atlantic near the Florida-Georgia line. Its great mouth is salt and tidal,
and ocean-going vessels steam into it as far as Jacksonville. It rises to a
chain of small lakes near the Florida east coast, south of Melbourne.

1. What kind of a selection do you think this is?

____

____

____

2. What might your purpose be for reading this selection? Why?

____

____

____

Below is a list of several different types of selections. What might be your
purpose for reading each of these types of selections? Explain why.

3. a novel

____

____

4. a comic book

____

____

5. a chapter on another country in a social studies textbook

____

____

6. a magazine article about a rock star

____

____

7. a recipe

____

____

NAME ____ DATE ___________

ACTIVE READING: QUESTION AND CLARIFY

Introduction

Question: Asking yourself questions while you read can help improve your reading comprehension. The first step is identifying what is confusing to you.

Clarify: You will probably find the answer to your question by stopping to think; looking back over material you have already read; or continuing to read on, keeping your question in mind. Sometimes, when the meaning of a word is the source of your confusion, looking up the word in a dictionary will help clarify the sentence or passage.

Question	Clarify
Establish specific point of confusion	Stop and think
Construct question	Reread confusing part Read ahead to see if new information clarifies confusing part

Model

Read the passage below from "The Parakeet Named Dreidel," by Isaac Bashevis Singer. Note the interrupter questions and answers in italics.

That night Dreidel slept on a picture frame and woke us in the morning with its singing. The bird stood on the frame, its plumage brilliant in the purple light of the rising sun, shaking as in prayer, whistling, twittering and talking all at the same time.

What is brilliant plumage? If you looked these words up in a dictionary, you would find plumage means a bird's feathers. Brilliant means sparkling or very splendid.

The parakeet must have belonged to a house where Yiddish was spoken because we heard it say "Zeldele, geh schlofen" (Zeldele, go to sleep), and these simple words uttered by the tiny creature filled us with wonder and delight.

What is Yiddish? I read on and found that Yiddish is a foreign language that the narrator can speak.

Practice

Below is another passage from "A Parakeet Named Dreidel," by Isaac Bashevis Singer. As you read the passage below, ask yourself questions about what is happening.

> The next day I posted a notice in the elevators of the neighborhood houses. It said that we had found a Yiddish-speaking parakeet. When a few days passed and no one called, I advertised in the newspaper for which I wrote, but a week went by and no one claimed the bird. Only then did Dreidel become ours. We bought a large cage with all the fittings and toys that a bird might want, but because Hanukkah is a festival of freedom, we resolved never to lock the cage. (The man at the pet shop had told us that the bird was a male.)

A. What were some questions you asked yourself while reading this passage? Write them and your answer in the space below. Tell how you arrived at your answer.

____

____

____

____

B. Challenge!
Select another passage from "A Parakeet Named Dreidel" or another piece of literature. As you read, write down questions that come to mind. Then try to answer those questions, and explain how you arrived at your answer.

____

____

____

____

ACTIVE READING: CONNECT

Introduction

Understanding what you read requires that you connect to the text in some way. Often, you will be reminded of something else you once read or you may have even had a similar personal experience to the one described. Everyone connects to a text in a completely unique and individual way. The way that you think about and connect to characters, events, comments, or descriptions in the text may be very different from the manner in which your friend connects to those things. Some of the connections you will likely have in common with your classmates, however, are the ones that you can make by connecting ideas within the text.

Here is a helpful list of the various ways that you can actively connect to a text as you read:

- Connect what is said with your own ideas or feelings.
- Connect what is described with experiences from your own life.
- Connect what is said with other texts such as stories or articles that you have read.
- Connect the ideas, characters, events, or descriptions within the text to each other.

Model

The passage below is from "The Osage Orange," by William Stafford. As you read it, make your own connections. Some typical connections you might make are listed below.

> On that first day of high school in the prairie town where the tree was, I stood in the sun by the flagpole and watched, but pretended not to watch, the others. They stood in groups and talked and knew each other, all except one—a girl though—in a faded blue dress, carrying a sack lunch and standing near the corner looking everywhere but at the crowd. I might talk to her, I thought. But of course it was out of the question.
>
> That first day was easier when the classes started. Some of the teachers were kind; some were frightening. Some of the students didn't care, but I listened and waited; and at the end of the day I was relieved, less conspicuous from then on.

If asked, a person may mention these types of connections:

- personal memories and thoughts of the first day of high school
- the familiar image of a flagpole
- the experience of feeling alone or watching others talk
- how the narrator is separated from the others

Practice

Below is another passage from "The Osage Orange." As you read the
selection, think about how you connect to it.

> As I hurried to carry my new paper route, I was thinking about how in
> a strange town, if you are quiet, no one notices, and someone may like
> you, later. I was thinking about this when I reached the north edge of
> town where the scattering houses dwindle. Beyond them to the north lay
> just openness, the plains, a big swoop of nothing. There, at the last house,
> just as I cut across a lot and threw to the last customer, I saw the girl in
> the blue dress coming along the street, heading on out of town, carrying
> books. And she saw me.
>
> "Hello."
>
> "Hello."
>
> And because we stopped, we were friends. I didn't know how I could
> stop, but I didn't hurry on. There was nothing to do but to act as if I were
> walking on out too. I had three papers left in the bag, and I frantically
> began to fold them—box them, as we called it—for throwing. We had
> begun to walk and talk. The girl was timid; I became more bold. Not
> much, but a little.
>
> "Have you gone to school here before?" I asked.
>
> "Yes, I went here last year."

Now make a list of the ideas, comments, or descriptions from the passage
that you connect to. Write down even the most simple connections that
you have. Also consider how aspects of the passage relate to each other.
Then briefly describe the connections in the space provided.

	Phrase from the Passage	Connection
1.		
2.		
3.		
4.		
5.		
6.		
7.		

ACTIVE READING: KWL

Introduction

By determining how you will read and thinking about what you read,
you can become an active reader. Whether you read a story or a work of
nonfiction, you may want to use a strategy known as **KWL** to get the
most out of a selection. The letters *KWL* stand for *Know, Want,* and *Learn.*
To use the KWL strategy, follow these steps:

- Brainstorm what you *know* about the subject before you read.
  Think about facts and details.
- Before you read, list what you *want* to learn as a result of
  reading the selection. Write down questions that you have
  about this subject. You may want to find answers to such
  questions as *who?, what?, where?, when?, why?,* and *how?*
- After you finish reading, evaluate what you have *learned* about
  this subject. List new information you gained as a result of
  your reading.

Model

You may want to use a chart like the one shown below to help you
organize what you already know about a subject, what you want to learn,
and what you learn as a result of your reading.

K (What I **Know**)	W (What I **Want to Learn**)	L (What I **Learned**)

Reading Tips

- Jot down these questions in order to help you remember the
  steps involved in using the KWL strategy: What do I <u>K</u>now?
  What do I <u>W</u>ant to learn? What did I <u>L</u>earn?
- Before you read a selection, list what you already know about a
  subject. Then list what you want to find out about the subject
  in the form of questions. As you read, look for the answers to
  these questions.
- If your questions about a subject were not answered in the
  reading, use different sources of information—encyclopedias,
  people in the community, textbooks—to help you answer them.

NAME _______________________________ **DATE** ___________

Practice

Below is a passage about Nate Archibald, a former professional basketball player. Before you read, fill in the first two columns of the KWL chart. First, write what you know about Nate Archibald. Then write what you want to learn about him. Then read the passage. After you finish, write what you learned.

Like countless city kids, Tiny Archibald grew up dreaming of playing pro basketball. It's a low-percentage dream. There are so few jobs in the National Basketball Association, and so many hungry applicants. Even boys who grow up in ghettos have a far better chance to become doctors or lawyers than they do to compete in the NBA. And even the ones who make it to the pros often have careers that last only a few years.

But the logic of numbers couldn't compete with the glamour of the dream for the young Archibald, who early on inherited the nickname "Tiny" from his father. Tiny wanted to play the game he loved against the very best. And he coupled his dream with a dedication that few of his fellow ballplayers could match. Even his mother was astonished by Tiny's determination and by the way it drove his concentration on the game. "It's just as though he was in a cave, and all that was in the cave was a basketball and a hoop," she told John Devaney, who wrote a book about Tiny years later.

In his cave, Tiny was focused and safe. As a little boy in the South Bronx, he played basketball each day after school. If the gym was open, he played indoors as long as there were ten guys there to make up two teams. After everybody else went home, Tiny stayed around and popped jump shots by himself until the janitor told him it was time to lock up. Then he went outside and fired away at the basket on the asphalt court outside. The rim was bent and somebody had stolen the net, but it was still a basket. Tiny would practice until it was too dark to see whether his shots were going in or not. Then he'd dribble the ball he'd borrowed from the coach all the way home. He'd practice dribbling behind his back and between his legs, moves that required concentration enough so that he didn't have to notice the garbage and wrecked cars in the streets.

Nate "Tiny" Archibald		
K (What I **Know**)	**W** (What I **Want to Learn**)	**L** (What I **Learned**)

IDENTIFY MAIN IDEA AND SUPPORTING DETAILS

Introduction

Effective readers look for the most important point a writer is trying to make. This helps them create meaning, or make sense, of the text. The central idea in a passage is its **main idea**. The main idea can appear at the beginning, middle, or end of a passage. There are two types of main ideas.

- A **stated main idea** is one in which the main idea of the passage is stated clearly in one sentence in the selection.
- An **implied main idea** is not stated in any one sentence. Instead, it is revealed indirectly through the connections among the details in the passage.

Writers support main ideas with **supporting details.** When you are reading, it is important to recognize these words, phrases, or sentences that tell something about the main idea. They can be facts, statistics, dates, names, opinions, or details.

Model

Look for the main idea and supporting details in this passage. Compare your answers to the ones below:

> My younger sister Doris, though two years younger than I, had enough gumption for a dozen people. She positively enjoyed washing dishes, making beds, and cleaning the house. When she was only seven she could carry a piece of short-weighted cheese back to the A&P, threaten the manager with legal action, and come back triumphantly with the full quarter pound we'd paid for and a few ounces extra thrown in for forgiveness.

Main Idea

- My younger sister Doris, though two years younger than I, had enough gumption for a dozen people.

This sentence clearly states the central idea of the paragraph, that Doris had a lot of gumption. This is the idea the writer wants to get across to the reader.

Supporting Details

- She enjoyed washing dishes, making beds, and cleaning the house.
- She had the guts to get her money's worth from the supermarket.

These details are examples that support and illustrate the main idea. The writer is not specifically interested in telling the reader a story about his sister and housework or the A&P. He does so strictly to give weight to his assertion of her gumption.

NAME ________________________   **DATE** __________

Practice

Part I

Below is a passage from "I Learn to Speak," from *The Story of My Life*, by Helen Keller. Read the passage and answer the questions that follow.

> It was in the spring of 1890 that I learned to speak. The impulse to utter audible sounds had always been strong within me. I used to make noises, keeping one hand on my throat while the other hand felt the movements of my lips. I was pleased with anything that made a noise and liked to feel the cat purr and the dog bark. I also liked to keep my hand on a singer's throat, or on a piano when it was being played. Before I lost my sight and hearing, I was fast learning to talk, but after my illness it was found that I had ceased to speak because I could not hear. I used to sit in my mother's lap all day long and keep my hands on her face because it amused me to feel the motions of her lips; and I moved my lips, too, although I had forgotten what talking was. My friends say that I laughed and cried naturally, and for awhile I made many sounds and word-elements, not because they were a means of communication, but because the need for exercising my vocal organs was imperative. There was, however, one word the meaning of which I still remembered, water. I pronounced it "wa-wa." Even this became less and less intelligible until the time when Miss Sullivan began to teach me. I stopped using it only after I had learned to spell the word on my fingers.

1. What statement best expresses the main idea of this passage? Explain your answer.

   ____

   ____

   ____

   ____

2. Is the main idea implied or stated?

   ____

3. Identify five supporting details in this passage. Write the details in the spaces provided. Explain how each detail supports the main idea.

   1. ____

   2. ____

   3. ____

   4. ____

   5. ____

NAME ____   DATE _______________

Part II

Below is another passage from "I Learn to Speak," from *The Story of My Life*, by Helen Keller. Read the passage and answer the questions that follow.

> I had known for a long time that the people about me used a method of communication different from mine; and even before I knew that a deaf child could be taught to speak, I was conscious of dissatisfaction with the means of communication I already possessed. One who is entirely dependent upon the manual alphabet has always a sense of restraint, of narrowness. This feeling began to agitate me with a vexing, forward-reaching sense of a lack that should be filled. My thoughts would often rise and beat up like birds against the wind; and I persisted in using my lips and voice. Friends tried to discourage this tendency, fearing lest it would lead to disappointment. But I persisted, and an accident soon occurred which resulted in the breaking down of this barrier—I heard the story of Ragnhild Kaata.

1. What statement best expresses the main idea of this passage? Explain your answer.

   ____

   ____

   ____

   ____

2. Is the main idea implied or stated?

   ____

3. Identify the supporting details in this passage. Write the details in the spaces provided. Explain how each detail supports the main idea.

   1. ____

   2. ____

   3. ____

   4. ____

   5. ____

Part III

Below is a passage from "Sal Fink," by Robert D. San Souci. Read the passage and answer the questions that follow.

> Legendary Mississippi River boatman Mike Fink had one daughter, Sal, who was a "ring-tailed roarer" in her own right. In fact, she became known far and wide as the "Mississippi Screamer," because of the way she would bellow *"Hi-i-i-i-i-ow-ow-ow-who-whooh!"* when she was feeling high-spirited or ready for a fight. Up and down the river she was known for fighting a duel with a thunderbolt, riding the river on the back of an alligator while "standen upright an' dancing 'Yankee Doodle'," and even outracing a steamboat poling her own keelboat with a handpicked crew.

1. What statement best expresses the main idea of this passage? Explain your answer.

   ____

   ____

   ____

   ____

2. Is the main idea implied or stated?

   ____

3. Identify the supporting details in this passage. Write the details in the spaces provided. Explain how each detail supports the main idea.

   1. ____

   2. ____

   3. ____

   4. ____

   5. ____

MAKE INFERENCES

Introduction

An **inference** is a reasonable guess or logical conclusion. Making inferences allows you to figure out things that aren't explicitly stated. Effective readers make inferences all the time as they read. They think carefully about the information they are given and combine it with their own knowledge about people and life in general. From this combination they are able to make inferences or logical conclusions that help them to understand the text. Although you may often make inferences naturally, at other times you may need to read between the lines and think about what is said.

Helpful Hint

Keep this equation in mind to understand how you make inferences:

Textual clues   +   What You Know   =   Inference

Model

Read the passage below from "Ginger for the Heart," by Paul Yee. Then see if the inferences you made match the ones listed below.

> Yenna had little to give him in farewell. All she found in the kitchen was a ginger root as large as her hand. As she stroked its brown knobs and bumpy eyes, she whispered to him. "This will warm you in the cold weather. I will wait for you, but, like this piece of ginger, I too will age and grow dry." Then she pressed her lips to the ginger, and turned away. "I will come back," the young man said. "The fire burning for you in my heart can never be extinguished."

Inference: Yenna is not wealthy and she doesn't have many possessions.
Support for this inference: *The passage says that Yenna had little to give him. All she found was ginger root.*

Inference: The man will be gone for a long time.
Support for this inference: *She says she will wait but she will age at the same time. This indicates that she doesn't expect his return soon.*

Inference: The man loves her.
Support for this inference: *He says the fire in his heart will never die.*

Practice

Below is another passage from "Ginger for the Heart." Read it and then practice making inferences by using the chart below.

Thereafter, Yenna lit a lamp at every nightfall and set it in the tower window. Rains lashed against the glass, snow piled low along the ledge and ocean winds rattled the frame. But the flame did not waver, even though the young man never sent letters. Yenna did not weep uselessly, but continued to sew and sing with her mother.

One day a dusty traveler came into the store and flung a bundle of ragged clothes onto the counter. Yenna shook out the first shirt and rolled out a ginger root. Taking it into her hand, she saw that pieces had been nibbled off, but the core of the root was still firm and fragrant.

Make five different inferences about this passage by using this chart.

Textual Clues	+	What You Know	=	Inference
1. Yenna lit a lamp at every nightfall				
2. Rains lashed against the glass, snow piled low along the ledge, and ocean winds rattled the frame.				
3. Yenna did not weep uselessly, but continued to sew and sing with her mother.				
4. . . . a dusty traveler came into the store and flung a bundle of ragged clothes onto the counter.				
5. Yenna shook out the first shirt and rolled out a ginger root.				

B. Challenge!

Besides when you are reading, think of other situations when you need to make inferences.

____

Why is the ability to make inferences so important?

____

COMPARE AND CONTRAST

Introduction

As you read, look for the writer's use of comparisons and contrasts. A writer uses **comparison** to show how things are similar and uses **contrast** to show how things are different. Recognizing comparisons and contrast will help you identify the relationship between the people, places, and things you encounter in your reading.

Reading Tip

Look for clue words that may help you recognize a comparison or contrast. Clue words that may signal a comparison are *like, similar to,* and *the same.* Clue words that may signal a contrast are *but, different from,* and *however.*

Model

In the passage below from "Gentleman of Río en Medio," by Juan A. A. Sedillo, look for the ways which the writer, through using comparisons and contrasts, shows how the old man aspires to be a rich and powerful gentleman but falls short.

> The day of the sale he came into the office. His coat was old, green and faded. I thought of Senator Catron, who had been such a power with these people up there in the mountains. Perhaps it was one of his old Prince Alberts. He also wore gloves. They were old and torn and his fingertips showed through them. He carried a cane, but it was only the skeleton of a worn-out umbrella. Behind him walked one of his innumerable kin—a dark young man with eyes like a gazelle.

Comparison

- He carries a cane.
- He has a servant.

These descriptions show how the old man is similar to a gentleman.

Contrast

- He wears hand-me-down clothes that have become shabby.
- His cane is an umbrella.
- His servant is just a boy who is a relative.

These descriptions show how the old man is different from a gentleman.

Clue Word

but (He carried a cane, <u>but</u> it was only the skeleton of a worn-out umbrella.)
   The word *but* signals a contrast.

Practice

Below is another passage from "Gentleman of Río en Medio," by Juan A. A. Sedillo. Read the passage and answer the questions that follow. Note that the old man sees himself one way, and the writer sees him another way.

> The old man bowed to all of us in the room. Then he removed his hat and gloves, slowly and carefully. Chaplin once did that in a picture, in a bank— he was the janitor. Then he handed his things to the boy, who stood obediently behind the old man's chair.

1. Considering the old man's actions and the boy's behavior, to what kind of person would you compare the old man? Explain your answer.

   ____

   ____

2. With whom does the writer compare the old man? What does this comparison suggest about the old man?

   ____

   ____

   ____

3. **Challenge!**
   Circle the clue words in the following sentences that help you recognize comparisons and contrasts. Some sentences may have more than one clue word. On a separate piece of paper, indicate if a comparison or a contrast is used. Explain what each comparison reveals about the old man. Then explain the overall impression of the old man created through this combination of comparisons.

   a. The old man is treated differently than the Americans.
   b. Even though he has the appearance of a man who has enough money not to work for a living, actually he is quite poor.
   c. He wore expensive gloves; however, they were old and torn.
   d. Although he was poor, he still had a great sense of honor.
   e. He does his best to appear like a gentleman.
   f. His manners were the same as that of a rich man.
   g. His hand-carved cane was similar to that of a rich man.
   h. Both the old man and Senator Catron had servants.
   i. Chaplin worked in a bank, but he was only the janitor.
   j. His coat was identical to that of Senator Catron.

NAME ____ **DATE** _____________

IDENTIFY STEPS IN A PROCESS
OR FOLLOW A SEQUENCE OF EVENTS

Introduction

To understand what you read, you need to figure out how events are connected. Events in our lives occur in a time order or **sequence of events.** This happens in stories as well. When you are reading, notice how writers provide clue words or phrases such as *first, second, finally, then, to begin with, later that night,* and so forth to indicate the passage of time.

Model

Look for the sequence of events in this passage. Notice that the author uses clue phrases such as *that first summer, and at dawn,* and *sell later* to indicate the passage of time or sequence of events.

> That first summer, their family had also gone smelting every night while the vast schools of fish were swimming upriver to spawn, and had caught enough to fill their freezer full of smelt. And at dawn, when the dew was still thick on the grass, they had also combed the golf course at the country club for nightcrawlers, filling up large buckets with worms that they would sell later to the roadside grocery stores as fishbait. The money from selling the worms enabled them to buy a hundred-pound sack of the best long-grain fragrant rice, and that, together with the frozen smelt and homegrown vegetables, had lasted them through the winter.

Practice

Read this passage and answer the questions that follow.

> . . . "Drive to the end of the street, and take a right," the test instructor said. He spoke in a low, bored staccato that Saeng had to strain to understand.
>
> Obediently she started up the car, careful to step on the accelerator very slowly, and eased the car out into the middle of the street. *Check the rearview mirror, make the hand gestures, take a deep breath,* Saeng told herself.
>
> So far, so good. At the intersection at the end of the street, she slowed down. Two cars were coming down the cross street toward her at quite a high speed. Instinctively, she stopped, and waited for them both to drive past. Instead, they both stopped, as if waiting for her to proceed.
>
> Saeng hesitated. Should she go ahead and take the turn before them or wait until they went past?
>
> Better to be cautious, she decided, and waited, switching gears over to neutral.
>
> For what seemed an interminable moment, nobody moved. Then the other cars went through the intersection, one after the other. Carefully, Saeng then took her turn *(turn signal, hand signal, look both ways).*

1. The author uses only one clue word to indicate the passage of time or sequence of events. What is it?

____

2. Without looking at the above passage, correctly number the sentences below according to their sequence.
   a. ______ At the intersection at the end of the street, she slowed down.
   b. ______ Obediently she started up the car.
   c. ______ Carefully, Saeng then took her turn.
   d. ______ Two cars were coming down the cross street toward her.
   e. ______ Instinctively, she stopped, and waited for them both to drive past.

B. Challenge!

3. Write about a typical day in your life beginning with waking up in the morning and going to bed at night. Remember that a sequence of events is a framework for organizing information for the purpose of telling a story. Use clue words and phrases such as *then, finally, later that day,* and so forth to indicate the passage of time.

____

____

____

____

RECOGNIZE SPATIAL RELATIONSHIPS

Introduction

Spatial order is the organization of details according to their arrangement in space as seen by an observer. For example, you might read a descriptive paragraph in which the Statue of Liberty is described from top to bottom or the Grand Canyon is described from side to side. When you read, it is important to recognize **spatial relationships** so that you can visualize what is being described.

When you read a descriptive passage, you may encounter any of these spatial relationships:

top to bottom	left to right	front to back
bottom to top	right to left	inside to outside
side to side	back to front	near to far

Transitional words and phrases, such as those listed below, often signal spatial relationships.

above	between	next to
across	down	over
behind	in the middle of	under
below	inside	up

Model

This passage is from "Across the Continent," by Charles A. Lindbergh. Look for different kinds of spatial relationships in the passage and notice the underlined transitional words and phrases that signal spatial relationships.

I've left the broad valleys <u>behind</u>. <u>Below</u>, I see only steep sides of mountains, sheering into narrow, night-locked ravines. There's not even a spot fit to crash on. But the use of more power is working. The engine sometimes runs for several minutes between coughing spells.

I'm over 13,000 feet now. I wonder if it's the Continental Divide—that long, snowcapped ridge, reaching to outer limits of the moonlight. I clear summits by about 500 feet. Those big dark patches, <u>farther down</u>, may mark the timber line.

The Rockies are <u>behind</u>. Mountains melted quickly into foothills, and foothills have rolled out into level plains. I see the lights of four villages, stringing north and south. They're probably tied together by a railroad. I ease my stick <u>forward</u> to lose altitude and reach a warmer air. Soon I'll be over the panhandle of Oklahoma, if I've not drifted north of route.

Practice

A. Below is another passage from Lindbergh's account. Read the passage and circle five transitional words and phrases that signal spatial relationships.

What a hopeless place for a forced landing! I look down on boulder-strewn mountain sides. The few bushes on that summit must root in crevices of rock. There's not a level area in sight to which I could glide in emergency. A pilot has to trust his engine above terrain like this. Of course I could have spiraled to greater height, and then held a gliding angle to some valley clearing; but in another twenty miles I'll be over desert on the eastern side. I want to make a fast flight to St. Louis. Why lose time safeguarding my plane through a few minutes of daylight when I'm to spend the entire night above canyons, lava beds, and cliffs?

At 4:30 the escorting planes dip their wings and turn back toward San Diego. To my right is Superstition Mountain; to my left, the San Jacinto peaks. Ahead, the coastal range breaks down into sharp-shadowed desert ridges.

A great valley stretches out before me, sun-scorched, sage-flecked, veined with dry, stony creek beds. Soft desert colors merge into one another until I'm not sure whether the sands are more yellow or pink. In the middle of this valley is the Salton Sea—a pale blue wash which seems to have neither depth nor wetness. My course lies directly across it, toward the crinkled Chocolate range beyond. Men have died of thirst traversing such burning wastes on foot or muleback. I glance at the two canteens hanging beside me in the cockpit. Suppose I'm forced down in the desert. Have I enough water to take me out?

I pass the winding Colorado River at 5:45, on course, and continue eastward above lengthening shadows and the weird rock formations of the Southwest. As Dean Blake predicted, I have a tail wind.

Sunset finds me over purple valleys, dusk-filled canyons, and silhouetted cliffs of Arizona, climbing steadily toward night. There are threads of steel on the ground below, barely visible in gathering twilight-tracks of the Santa Fe, and my last check point of the day.

B. Challenge!

On a separate piece of paper, write a brief description of your classroom, using transitional words and phrases to show spatial relationships.

NAME ____ **DATE** __________

RECOGNIZE CAUSE AND EFFECT

Introduction

A **cause** is an event, action, or feeling that produces a result. An **effect** is the result that's produced by a cause. Recognizing cause and effect relationships can help the reader follow a story.

Reading Tip
Look for clue words that may help you recognize cause and effect, such as *because, so, for this reason, therefore, consequently, since, unless,* and *that is why.*

Model

In this passage from "The Cremation of Sam McGee", by Robert Service, the writer and Sam McGee are traveling by foot with dog sleds over the Yukon. As you read, look for causes and effects and compare them to the ones below.

> And that very night, as we lay packed tight in our robes beneath the
>   snow,
> And the dogs were fed, and the stars o'erhead were dancing heel and
>   toe.
> He turned to me, and "Cap," says he, "I'll cash in this trip, I guess;
> And if I do, I'm asking that you won't refuse my last request."
> Well, he seemed so low that I couldn't say no; then he says with a sort
>   of moan:
> "It's the cursèd cold, and it's got right hold till I'm chilled clean through
>   the bone.
> Yet 'tain't being dead—it's my awful dread of the icy grave that pains;
> So I want you to swear that, foul or fair, you'll cremate my last remains."
> A pal's last need is a thing to heed, so I swore I would not fail . . . .

Cause
- Sam McGee feels he's going to die.

This statement shows the feeling that produces a result.

Effect
- Sam McGee requests that his body be cremated.

This statement shows the result produced by a feeling.

Cause
- The writer feels that he can't refuse a friend's last request.

This statement shows the feeling that produces a result.

Effect
- The writer promises to cremate Sam McGee when he dies.

This statement shows the result produced by a feeling.

Practice

Below is another passage from "The Cremation of Sam McGee," by
Robert Service. Read the passage and answer the questions that follow.

> Some planks I tore from the cabin floor, and I lit the boiler fire;
> Some coal I found that was lying around, and I heaped the fuel higher;
> The flames just soared, and the furnace roared—such a blaze you seldom see;
> And I burrowed a hole in the glowing coal, and I stuffed in Sam McGee.
>
> Then I made a hike, for I didn't like to hear him sizzle so;
> And the heavens scowled, and the huskies howled, and the wind began
> to blow.

1. What causes Sam McGee's friend to hike?

____

2. What effect does this have?

____

____

____

3. In the sentences below, circle the clue words or phrases that help you
   recognize cause and effect. Explain how each word or phrase helps to
   clue you in to a cause-effect relationship.
   a. The Arctic Circle is extremely cold. For this reason, I prefer to
      vacation in the Bahamas.

   ____

   ____

   b. Because he is an honorable man, he kept his promise.

   ____

   ____

   c. We were very cold. So we gathered wood and built a fire.

   ____

   ____

   d. Since he was my friend, I had to grant his last wish.

   ____

   ____

   e. We needed the dogs to pull the sleds; therefore, we always made
      sure the dogs were fed.

   ____

   ____

NAME ___________________________ DATE __________

IDENTIFY PROBLEMS AND SOLUTIONS

Introduction

Identifying the problem and solution in a text will give you a better appreciation of what you are reading. **Problems** are the challenges that people encounter. **Solutions** are the answers to those problems. As you read a text, you will often find that there is a central problem but there may also exist many smaller problems that need to be solved. Various steps or actions may be taken to solve the problems before a final solution is reached.

Model

In a nonfiction selection such as "Lego," by David Owen, the text is structured specifically to introduce the problem and explore how the solution was arrived at.

Read the passage below from "Lego" and concentrate on identifying Francie Berger's problems and solutions. See if your ideas match the chart below.

> Growing up in Queens in the sixties and seventies, Francie Berger knew exactly what she wanted from life: more Lego building bricks. She received her first set, a gift from her parents, when she was three. Gradually, she added to her holdings. She liked to build houses, and she wished that she could build bigger ones. As a teen-ager, she began writing to Lego Systems, Inc., the American division of the toy's Danish manufacturer, to ask if she could order, say, two million standard red bricks. The company said that she could not. In college—where she majored in architecture, figuring that building real houses was the adult occupation that came closest to her favorite activity—she wrote more letters. At some point, it occurred to her that she might be able to get a job at Lego itself. She began calling the company on a monthly basis, and she once dropped by its head-quarters in Enfield, Connecticut . . . . Undeterred she spent part of her senior year using Lego bricks to build a scale model of a farm. The model served both as her senior thesis and as a job application. Seeing no way out, Lego hired her, in 1984, for a three-week trial period. She has been with the company ever since . . . .

Problem	Steps to Solve the Problem	Solution
She wants more bricks.	She writes to Lego.	none
She wants a job with Lego.	• She calls monthly. • She drops by the head-quarters. • She applies for a job.	She gets hired for a three-week trial period.

Comprehension STRATEGY

Practice

Read the passage below, which is another excerpt from "Lego." Keep in mind the first passage you read as well and then answer the following questions.

> While Berger and her colleague worked, people gathered around to watch and ask questions. Many of the people wanted to know what they would have to do to get a job at Lego. Every year Berger receives dozens of letters from children, art students, engineers, architects, and others, all wanting to know the same thing. "A lot of kids ask what kind of college courses they should take," Berger told us. "When I write back, I just kind of explain how I got my job. It was a little unorthodox, but it worked for me."
>
> Berger's job didn't exist when she was hired. At that time, all the models used by Lego's American division were made in Denmark and shipped to the United States. To Berger, that seemed nutty. Why not build those models right here in America, and why not let Francie Berger build them? Today, she supervises two other designers and half a dozen full-time model-builders. All these people are, in effect, manifestations of her determination to spend her life doing the things she likes best.

1. How does Francie Berger go about solving her problem of finding a way to always be involved in Lego building?

   ____

   ____

2. A lot of people are interested in working for Lego and write to Francie Berger for advice. Do you think she gives them solutions? Why or why not?

   ____

   ____

3. What aspect of the way Lego operates does Francie Berger believe is a problem? How does she solve it?

   ____

   ____

4. What character traits does Francie Berger have that make her a good problem solver?

   ____

   ____

NAME ____ DATE __________

USE VISUAL AND GRAPHIC CLUES

Introduction

Knowing when and how to use visual and graphic sources of information is an important skill to master when you are reading. Visual and graphic sources of information may present facts and details that will help you better understand what you read. Some examples of visual and graphic sources of information that you will use are listed below.

diagrams	lists	maps
illustrations	scale drawings	schedules
tables	timelines	graphs
charts	diagrams	cartoons

A *schedule* is one kind of visual or graphic source of information that you use to find out when certain events take place. For example, you may want to use a schedule to find out when a certain movie is playing at the local theater, when a documentary you are interested in will air on TV, or when the city bus runs on Sunday. The information in a schedule is arranged in rows and columns. Headings tell you what information is given in each column or row. The information given in a schedule may consist of words, numbers, and symbols.

Model

Study this example of a schedule to discover what happened to explorer Thor Heyerdahl when his wooden raft washed onto a coral reef.

Record of Events on Day *Kon-Tiki* Washed Up onto Coral Reef	
Time	**Event**
6:00 A.M.	Line of small islands sighted
7:30 A.M.	Exactly seven islands spotted to the west
8:15 A.M.	Approach to islands close enough to see separate palm trees
8:45 A.M.	Wind still, a wreck sighted on reef
9:50 A.M.	Reef seen to be approximately 100 yards away
9:55 A.M.	Anchor overboard, catches hold of bottom

Reading Tips

- Remember that visual and graphic sources of information are pictorial representations of information. You may have to interpret information that is given.
- If you encounter visual and graphic sources of information when you read, slow down. Visual and graphic sources of information may either provide information that will help you understand what you are reading or provide additional information that is not in the text.

NAME _______________________________   DATE _________

Practice

A. Use the train schedule below to answer the questions that follow.

Catskill to Aurora		Aurora to Catskill	
Departures	Arrivals	Departures	Arrivals
*6:30 A.M.	7:30 A.M.	*7:45 A.M.	6:30 A.M.
8:30 A.M.	9:40 A.M.	9:45 A.M.	10:55 A.M.
3:00 P.M.	4:10 P.M.	*4:25 P.M.	5:25 P.M.
*5:40 P.M.	6:40 P.M.	*6:55 P.M.	7:55 P.M.
*Nonstop service			

1. Which nonstop train leaving Catskill departs earliest in the morning?

   ____

2. If you must be in Aurora by 9:30 A.M., which train must you take
   from Catskill?

   ____

3. When would you arrive in Catskill if you left Aurora on the 6:55 P.M.
   train?

   ____

4. If you wanted to be in Catskill by 6:00 P.M., which train must you
   take from Aurora?

   ____

5. How long is the trip between Aurora and Catskill if you ride on a
   nonstop train?

   ____

B. Challenge!
Make a schedule to show when events in your life take place during a
typical day.

INTERPRET FIGURATIVE LANGUAGE

Introduction

Figurative language is language that goes beyond the literal meaning of words. Figurative language creates interesting and unusual comparisons that provide fresh ways of viewing the world by comparing unfamiliar objects and emotions to our own experience. Some common figures of speech are:

- **simile:** A comparison between two seemingly dissimilar things that uses *like* or *as*. (Example: "That sprinter runs like a deer.")
- **metaphor:** A comparison between two seemingly dissimilar things in which one thing is spoken of as if it were another. A metaphor doesn't use *like* or *as*. ("He's my sunshine in January.")
- **personification:** The granting of human qualities to nonhuman things. ("The rain laughed at my umbrella.") Hint: Personification usually involves active verbs.

Read the passage below, from "Forest Fire," by Anais Nin, with the underlined examples of figurative language.

> . . . The streets were blocked with (1) <u>fire engines readying to fight the fire</u> if it touched the houses. Policemen and firemen and guards turned away the sightseers. Some were relatives concerned over the fate of the foresters, or the pack station family. (2) <u>The policemen lighted flares, which gave the scene a theatrical, tragic air</u>. The red lights on the police cars twinkled alarmingly. More fire engines arrived. Ashes fell, and (3) <u>the roar of the fire was now like thunder</u>.

Notice the use of personification in sentence (1). The fire engines are given the human quality of being able to fight fires. In sentence (2), the scene at the fire is compared to the scene at a theater. Since this comparison does not use *like* or *as*, it is a metaphor. Sentence (3) contains a simile comparing the sound of the fire to the sound of thunder.

Practice

Below, you'll find another passage from "Forest Fire." Please read the
passage and underline all the examples of figurative language you can
find. Explain what type of figurative language each represents. Then tell
what each example adds to the piece of writing.

> But high above and all around, the fire was burning, more vivid than the
> sun, throwing spirals of smoke in the air like the smoke from a volcano.
> Thirty-three cabins burned, and twelve thousand acres of forest still burning
> endangered countless homes below the fire. The fire was burning to the back
> of us now, and a rain of ashes began to fall and continued for days . . . . The
> dragon tongues of flames devouring, the flames leaping, the roar of destruc-
> tion and dissolution, the eyes of the panicked animals, caught between fire
> and human beings, between two forms of death. They chose the fire. It was
> as if the fire had come from the bowels of the earth, like that of a fiery
> volcano, it was so powerful, so swift, and so ravaging. I saw trees become
> skeletons in one minute, I saw trees fall, I saw bushes turned to ashes in a
> second, I saw weary, ash-covered men, looking like men returned from war,
> some with burns, others overcome by smoke.

Challenge!

Select another passage from "Forest Fire" or another literature selection
that contains figurative language. Write examples of figurative language
you find in the space below. Explain what kind of figurative language
each is, and tell what it adds to the piece of literature.

____

____

____

____

____

____

____

NAME ____ DATE __________

DISTINGUISH BETWEEN IMPORTANT AND UNIMPORTANT INFORMATION

Introduction

An essential skill in critical reading is the ability to distinguish between important and less important information. With this skill, readers can concentrate on the key points that are worth remembering. Readers can use the strategy to identify important ideas in nonfiction: when reading a textbook, for example, or doing research for a report. It is also a useful strategy when reading fiction: to analyze story characters, setting, experiences, and events.

Here are some things to remember when you use the strategy:

Helpful Hints
- Read through the entire piece of writing before making decisions.
- Look for the *main idea* of a paragraph, passage, or text. Important information will always back up main ideas.
- Focus on the information that the *author* considers important.
- Identify details and ask yourself: "Should I remember this information?"
- Think about your decisions—why certain information is more important.

Some of the following ideas have checkmarks. These are important ideas for a report on the topic "Behavior of the Killer Whale." Can you explain why they are important and the others are less important?

> The killer whale inhabits all oceans.
> The killer whale is about 30 feet long and weighs as much as 8 tons.
> ✔ This kind of whale often hunts in packs.
> ✔ Killer whales prey on penguins, seals, dolphins, and other whales as well as fish.
> Killer whales have a black back and a white underside.
> ✔ The killer whale can swim extremely fast, as fast as 30 knots.
> ✔ It can dive to a depth of 3,000 feet.
> The killer whale has a dorsal fin.
> ✔ This whale can stay underwater for over 20 minutes.

The checks indicate information which directly bears upon the *behavior* of killer whales.

Practice

Below is a passage from "Coming into the Country," a nonfiction account written by John McPhee. After you read the passage, list the information you think you should remember and the information you think is less important. Explain your decisions.

> On a high promontory in the montane ruggedness around the upper Charley River lies the wreckage of an aircraft that is readily identifiable as a B-24. This was the so-called Liberator, a medium-range bomber built for the Second World War. The wreckage is in the dead center of the country, and I happened over it in a Cessna early in the fall of 1975, during a long and extremely digressive flight that began in Eagle and ended many hours later in Circle. The pilot of the Cessna said he understood that the crew of the Liberator had bailed out, in winter, and that only one man had survived. I asked around to learn who might know more than that—querying, among others, the Air Force in Fairbanks, the Gelvins, various old-timers in Circle and Central, some of the river people, and Margaret Nelson, in Eagle, who had packed parachutes at Ladd Field, in Fairbanks, during the war. There had been one survivor—everyone agreed. No one knew his name. He had become a symbol in the country, though, and was not about to be forgotten. It was said that he alone had come out—long after all had been assumed dead—because he alone, of the widely scattered crew, was experienced in wilderness, knew how to live off the land, and was prepared to deal with the hostile cold. Above all, he had found a cabin, during his exodus, without which he would have died for sure.

1. Important Information: **Reason for My Decision:**

_______________________________   _______________________________

_______________________________   _______________________________

_______________________________   _______________________________

_______________________________   _______________________________

_______________________________   _______________________________

2. Less Important Information: **Reason for My Decision:**

_______________________________   _______________________________

_______________________________   _______________________________

_______________________________   _______________________________

_______________________________   _______________________________

_______________________________   _______________________________

NAME _______________________________________ **DATE** ___________

DISTINGUISH BETWEEN FACT AND OPINION OR NONFACT

Introduction

Writers sometimes express an opinion as if it were a fact. Often an opinion may be supported by evidence and may appear to be factual. At times information may even be untrue, out of date, or based on a guess. It is important, therefore, that readers think about what they read and form judgments as to whether the information is fact, opinion, or nonfact.

To help you distinguish between fact and opinion or between fact and nonfact in your reading, remember the following distinctions:

- A **statement of fact** is a piece of information that is true and may be verified by direct observation or measurement.
- A **statement of opinion** expresses a belief or judgment about something. It cannot be verified. A **valid opinion** is an opinion which is supported by evidence.
- A **nonfact** is conjecture, or a guess. It cannot be verified. It may be proved to be false.

Helpful Hints

Explicit verbal cues often signal that a statement is not a fact but an opinion. These signal words include verbs such as *must* and *should*. Cues also include adjectives that state qualities such as *good, bad, best, important, beautiful.*

Model

Read this passage from "Pecos Bill: The Cyclone," by Harold W. Felton, and identify at least one fact, one opinion, and one nonfact. Compare your answers with the ones below.

> Widow Maker had put on a good show, bucking as no ordinary horse could ever buck. Then Bill undertook to show the gaits he had taught the palomino. Other mustangs at that time had only two gaits. Walking and running. Only Widow Maker could pace. But now Bill had developed and taught him other gaits. Twenty-seven in all.

Fact: Bill had taught Widow Maker twenty-seven gaits. This can be verified by direct observation or measurement.
Opinion: Widow Maker had put on a good show. *Good* is a signal word.
Nonfact: Only Widow Maker could pace. This is conjecture and cannot be verified. It could be proved false.

Practice

Part I

Here is another passage from "Pecos Bill: The Cyclone," by Harold W. Felton. Read it critically to distinguish between fact and opinion or nonfact. Fill in the chart.

One of Bill's greatest feats, if not the greatest feat of all time, occurred unexpectedly one Fourth of July. He had invented the Fourth of July some years before. It was a great day for the cowpunchers. They had taken to it right off like the real Americans they were. But the celebration had always ended on a dismal note. Somehow it seemed to be spoiled by a cyclone.

Bill had never minded the cyclone much. The truth is he rather liked it. But the other celebrants ran into caves for safety. He invented cyclone cellars for them. He even named the cellars. He called them "'fraid holes." Pecos wouldn't even say the word "afraid." The cyclone was something like he was. It was big and strong too. He always stood by musing pleasantly as he watched it.

A Statement of Fact	A Statement of Opinion	A Nonfact	How I Know

NAME _______________________________   **DATE** _____________

Part II

Answer the questions about the following passage taken from *These Were the Sioux,* by Mari Sandoz. Read the passage carefully, deciding whether statements are facts, opinions, or nonfacts.

> By the time Young One was six weeks old he was little trouble to anyone, either in the cradleboard propped against a tipi pole or riding a mother's back while she went about her work. He would be up there some of the time until he was a year old or more, out of harm's way, seeing all the world from the high place and unpossessed by the mother's eyes. Before Young One was two months old it was decided he must swim, "before he forget it," the older mother told us, by signs. I took my baby brother down to see this.
>
> The woman carried Young One into a quieter spot along the riverbank and with her hands under the chest and belly, she eased the boy into the shallow, tepid water until it came up around him. Then, suddenly, his sturdy legs began to kick and his arms to flail out. The next time he lasted a little longer, and by the third or fourth time the woman could take her hands away for a bit while he held his head up and dog paddled for himself.

1. What facts are given about Young One learning to swim?

____

____

2. How does the writer verify the facts?

____

____

3. What opinion is expressed in the passage?

____

____

4. Do you think it is a valid opinion? Why or why not?

____

____

5. What statement is a nonfact? Why?

____

____

   Distinguish Between Fact and Opinion or Nonfact

Part III

Below is another passage from *These Were the Sioux*, by Mari Sandoz. As you read the passage, make a judgment as to whether the information is fact, opinion, or nonfact. List your decisions below and explain your thinking.

> The young Indian learned to make his own decisions, take the responsibility for his actions at an incredibly early age. When the baby began to crawl no one cried, "No, no!" and dragged him back from the enticing red of the tipi fire coals. Instead, his mother or anyone near watched only that he did not burn up. "One must learn from the bite of the fire to let it alone," he was told when he jerked his hand back, whimpering a little, and with tear-wet face brought his burnt finger to whoever was near for the soothing. The boy's eyes would not turn in anger toward the mother or other grownup who might have pulled him back, frustrated his natural desire to test, to explore. His anger was against the pretty coals, plainly the source of his pain. He would creep back another time but more warily, and soon he would discover where warmth became burning.

Fact

____

____

____

____

Opinion

____

____

____

____

Nonfact

____

____

____

____

EVALUATE AUTHOR'S PURPOSE AND POINT OF VIEW

Introduction

An **author's purpose** is the main reason that he or she has for writing a particular work of fiction or nonfiction. An author's purpose may be one of the following:

- to entertain
- to persuade
- to describe
- to inform

Many works of fiction or nonfiction have more than one purpose. When you are reading, remember an article that is written to persuade readers to recycle might also inform people about the recycling programs that currently exist in their communities. It might also describe how kitchen scraps can be recycled through the process of composting. Being able to recognize why an author has written a particular piece will help you to determine how you will read it and to better appreciate what you read.

Whether an author's purpose is to entertain, describe, inform, or persuade, the perspective that he or she takes when writing is called **point of view**. When you read nonfiction, the author's point of view is his or her opinions or attitudes toward a subject. By reading a selection carefully and by noting details, you can draw conclusions about an author's feelings concerning the subject that he or she is writing about.

When you read fiction, the author chooses a point of view from which to tell the story. An author may tell a story from **first-person** or **third-person** point of view. In both cases, the narrator, or teller of the story, is fictional. Study the chart below to learn about the differences between these two points of view.

Who Tells the Story?	
First Person	**Third Person**
A character in the story gives you his or her firsthand account of people and events, using the pronouns *I, me,* and *we*.	A narrator who is not one of the characters in the story tells what happens, using the pronouns *he, she,* and *it*.
Readers learn only what one character—the narrator—sees, thinks, and feels.	Readers may learn what one character or several characters in the story see, think, feel.

NAME _________________________________   **DATE** ___________

Practice

A. Complete the chart below by writing two examples of different types of writing whose purposes are to entertain, describe, persuade, or inform. The chart has been started for you.

Entertain	Describe	Persuade	Inform
story	travel brochure	editorial	encyclopedia article

B. Read the passage below from "Raymond's Run," a story by Toni Cade Bambara. Then complete the sentences that follow.

I don't have much work to do around the house like some girls. My mother does that. And I don't have to earn my pocket money by hustling: George runs errands for the big boys and sells Christmas cards. And anything else that's got to get done, my father does. All I have to do in life is mind my brother Raymond, which is enough.

Sometimes I slip and say my little brother Raymond. But as any fool can see he's much bigger and he's older too. But a lot of people call him my little brother cause he needs looking after cause he's not quite right. And a lot of smart mouths got lots to say about that too, especially when George was minding him. But now, if anybody has anything to say to Raymond, anything to say about his big head, they have to come by me. And I don't play the dozens[1] or believe in standing around with somebody in my face doing a lot of talking. I much rather just knock you down and take my chances even if I am a little girl with skinny arms and a squeaky voice, which is how I got the name Squeaky. And if things get too rough, I run. And as anybody can tell you, I'm the fastest thing on two feet.

---

1. the dozens: A game in which the players insult one another; the first to show anger loses.

1. The author's purpose is to____

2. The point of view from which the passage is told is ________________

____

3. This point of view reveals the thoughts and feelings of the following

character or characters: _______________________________________

____

NAME _______________________________   DATE ____________

EVALUATE EVIDENCE AND SOURCES OF INFORMATION

Introduction

Writers have many reasons for presenting evidence. Whatever the reason for its use, it's up to you to evaluate the reliability of pieces of evidence.

In order to evaluate the evidence, you'll have to think about its source. Is it the result of objective research? Did it come from historical documents or scholarly works? Was it drawn from interviews that include the interviewees' subjective emotions and opinions? Is it part of the author's life experience? Only when you've tried to answer these questions will you know how to evaluate the evidence presented in order to draw conclusions about what you are reading.

Keep track of the evidence you encounter by creating a chart like this:

Evidence	Probable Source	Fact or Opinion?

Model

Consider the evidence in this passage. Where do you think the author got this information? From the tone of the passage, do you think it was carefully researched? Compare your answers to the ones below.

> According to the findings of Dr. W. Fewkes, Dr. M. W. Stirling, and Dr. W. Sears, the habitation of Weedon Island began as early as 400 A.D. by mound builders, also called shell men. The mounds were utilized by these shell men and Timicuan-related Muskhogeans until the arrival of the Spanish in the sixteenth century. The only remainders of what archaeologists term the Weedon Island Cultures exist in their burial mounds and kitchen middens—mounds where they threw their shells, broken pottery, and old tools.
>
> In 1974, Weedon Island became Weedon Island State Preserve after it was purchased by the state under the Environmentally Endangered Lands Act.
>
> According to Blue Sky, a local Mohawk Indian and activist in the preservation of Weedon Island, although the island was a state preserve, it was not protected.
>
> "The state bought the island and called it a preserve and did nothing out here," said Blue Sky. "They just bought it and left it as it was."

Evidence	Probable Source	Fact or Opinion?
Habitation began 400 A.D.	3 researchers	fact?
State purchased in 1974	gov. record?	fact
Island was not protected by state	Blue Sky	opinion

NAME _______________________________________   **DATE** ____________

Practice

Below is another passage from "Weedon." Evaluate the evidence it presents by answering the questions.

Concern for the island and its historical landmarks intensified when the state announced plans to transform Weedon Island State Preserve into recreational area. American Indians were outraged by the plan. Afraid that the new proposal would not offer adequate protection for the mounds, they began a crusade to restore and preserve Weedon Island's natural habitat and culture.

According to Blue Sky, it was then that concerned people came together to protect the preserve. Community leaders, politicians, environmentalists and residents formed the Weedon Island Advisory Committee.

"Part of what we did was analyze what the current situation was," said City Commissioner Barbara Sheen Todd, head of the committee. "We found that the Indian mounds were being disturbed and that they were not protected adequately and that, in fact, the staff was not adequate. We found that boats were coming in there and tearing up the mudflats, that destroys the environmental basis for much of the life cycle. The community created the problem; the people were loving Weedon Island to death."

1. What evidence is presented to show that Weedon Island Preserve was being harmed? Give two instances:

   a. ____

   b. ____

2. What is the source of the evidence you listed in response to question 1?

   ____

3. Were the American Indians right to worry about the plan to turn Weedon Island into a recreational area? Cite evidence from the passage to support your answer.

   ____

   ____

4. After the Indians complained about the use of Weedon Island, government investigators sought more evidence. What did they find?

   ____

   ____

5. Which evidence about a place would you be more likely to believe? Evidence from people who live there or evidence from government studies? Explain your answer.

   ____

   ____

　　　　

NAME ____ DATE ___________

EVALUATE AUTHOR'S BIAS

Introduction

Two writers tackling the same subject are likely to come up with vastly different texts. Even if the facts are the same, the feelings, opinions, and claims expressed aren't likely to match. As you read, try to identify the writer's position or point of view. What special stakes does he or she have in a particular subject? What bias might cause the author to adopt a certain point of view?

It might help to put yourself through a three-step process in order to evaluate the author's bias.

Step 1: Who is the author? What is his or her relationship to the subject being discussed?

Step 2: Which details are facts? Which are opinions?

Step 3: What bias is revealed by the author's opinions?

$$\text{Opinion 1} \quad + \quad \text{Opinion 2} \quad + \quad \text{Opinion 3} \quad = \quad \text{What bias?}$$

Model

Read the following passage from "How to Enjoy Poetry," by James Dickey. Keep in mind that Dickey himself is a poet. Then separate facts from opinions in the essay. Finally, try to determine the author's bias in discussing the subject. Compare your results to those listed below.

> Where Poetry Is Coming From
>
> From the beginning, people have known that words and things, words and actions, words and feelings, go together, and that they can go together in thousands of different ways, according to who is using them. Some ways go shallow, and some go deep.
>
> Your Connection with Other Imaginations
>
> The first thing to understand about poetry is that it comes to you from outside you, in books or in words, but that for it to live, something from within you must come to it and meet it and complete it. Your response with your own mind and body and memory and emotions gives the poem its ability to work its magic; if you give to it, it will give to you and give plenty.
>
> When you read, don't let the poet write down to you; read up to him. Reach for him from your gut out, and the heart and muscles will come into it, too.

Step 1: Who is writing about the subject of poetry? A poet.

Step 2: The facts? **(a)** People have always known that words, things, actions, and feelings can go together. **(b)** Poetry comes to us from the outside, in books or words.

The Opinions? **(a)** Poetry creates a new part of you. **(b)** Poetry must be reached with heart and muscles.

Step 3: Bias of the author? He is a poet who has his own subjective ideas about how poetry works and how it should be read.

NAME _________________________________ DATE ___________

Practice

Below is another passage from "How to Enjoy Poetry." Read it, and then answer the questions that follow.

Which Sun? Whose Stars?

The sun is new every day, the ancient philosopher Heraclitus said. The sun of poetry is new every day, too, because it is seen in different ways by different people who have lived under it, lived with it, responded to it. Their lives are different from yours, but by means of the special spell that poetry brings to the fact of the sun—everybody's sun; yours, too— you can come into possession of many suns: as many as men and women have ever been able to imagine. Poetry makes possible the deepest kind of personal possession of the world.

The most beautiful constellation in the winter sky is Orion, which ancient poets thought looked like a hunter, up there, moving across heaven with his dog Sirius. What is this hunter made out of stars hunting for? What does he mean? Who owns him, if anybody? The poet Aldous Huxley felt that he did, and so, in Aldous Huxley's universe of personal emotion, he did.

> Up from among the emblems of the
>   wind into its heart of power,
> The Huntsman climbs, and all his
>   living stars
> Are bright, and all are mine.

1. Name at least one fact presented in this selection.

   ____

2. Name at least two opinions expressed in this selection.

   ____

   ____

3. Suppose this passage was written by someone who thinks that poems are usually too vague and too boring. Pick two sentences from the passage and rewrite them from that person's particular bias.

   a. ____

   b. ____

4. Does this passage express your attitude toward poetry? How is your attitude different from or similar to James Dickey's?

   ____

5. Explain your attitude in terms of your own bias. In other words, what experiences have influenced you to take this point of view?

   ____

DRAW CONCLUSIONS

Introduction

All writing does not always spell out conclusions. It's up to you to gather evidence and **draw conclusions** from it. In the case of persuasive essays, your conclusions might have something to do with whether you agree with the author. In the case of stories or novels, the evidence might lead to a conclusion about how a situation turned out or what a character is like. No matter what the kind of conclusions, the important thing is that they be based on facts and ideas presented.

As you read, try to jot down some of the conclusions you come to. Then list the facts that helped you arrive at them. You might use this form to record your conclusions and supporting facts.

Conclusion: ____

Facts: ____

Model

Read this passage from "If I Forget Thee, Oh Earth . . . ," by Arthur C. Clarke. What are your conclusions about what is happening? What facts back up these conclusions? Compare your answers to those below.

> Why could they not return? It seemed so peaceful beneath those lines of marching cloud. Then Marvin, his eyes no longer blinded by the glare, saw that the portion of the disk that should have been in darkness was gleaming faintly with an evil phosphorescence: and he remembered. He was looking upon the funeral pyre of a world—upon the radioactive aftermath of Armageddon. Across a quarter of a million miles of space, the flow of dying atoms was still visible, a perennial reminder of the ruinous past. It would be centuries yet before the deadly glow died from the rocks and life could return again to fill that silent, empty world.
>
> And now Father began to speak, telling Marvin the story which until this moment had meant no more to him than the fairy tales he had once been told. There were many things he could not understand: it was impossible for him to picture the glowing, multicolored pattern of life on the planet he had never seen. Nor could he comprehend the forces that had destroyed it in the end, leaving the Colony, preserved by its isolation, as the sole survivor.

Conclusion: Marvin is seeing a planet that has been devastated by a nuclear explosion.
Facts: Planet has "evil phosphorescence"; and is "funeral pyre of a world."
Conclusion: Marvin and Father may be part of the sole surviving colony of this planet.
Facts: Marvin had always known the story of the planet; the Colony was the sole surviving group from the planet; Marvin and Father seem to be a part of this colony.

NAME _______________________________ **DATE** _______________

Practice

Read this next passage from "If I Forget Thee, Oh Earth . . . ," by Arthur C. Clarke. Cross out the conclusions that are incorrect. List the supporting facts under the correct conclusions.

> . . . About a mile ahead Marvin could see the curiously shaped structures clustering round the head of a mine. Now and then a puff of vapor would emerge from a squat smokestack and would instantly disperse.
>
> They were past the mine in a moment. Father was driving with a reckless and exhilarating skill as if—it was a strange thought to come into a child's mind—he were trying to escape from something. In a few minutes they had reached the edge of the plateau on which the Colony had been built. The ground fell sharply away beneath them in a dizzying slope whose lower stretches were lost in shadow. Ahead, as far as the eye could reach, was a jumble wasteland of craters, mountain ranges, and ravines. The crests of the mountains, catching the low sun, burned like islands of fire in the sea of darkness: and above them the stars still shone as steadfastly as ever.

1. **Conclusion:** Marvin and his father set off a mine explosion.

   Facts: ____

   ____

   ____

2. **Conclusion:** There was a possibility that Marvin and Father might have a driving accident.

   Facts: ____

   ____

   ____

3. **Conclusion:** Marvin and Father were driving along the edge of a steep drop.

   Facts: ____

   ____

   ____

4. **Conclusion:** Marvin's father was taking him to the headquarters of the Colony.

   Facts: ____

   ____

   ____

　　　

SUMMARIZE

Introduction

Effective readers know how to **summarize.** The process starts when you separate important and unimportant information in your reading. You can then condense it into a form that can easily be remembered for retelling or rewriting. Follow these tips:
- Read the passage.
- Identify important information.
- Condense the information for easy recall.

Model

Read the passage below. As you read, think about the main ideas of the passage. Then compare your ideas with the sample summary given below. Notice that the summary gives only a bare outline of Mallory and Farrar's exchange, in the order that it happened. Details such as Mallory's brusqueness are omitted. However, the summary provides a good overall sense of what happened during the exchange.

> The older professor looked up at the assistant, fumbling fretfully with a pile of papers. "Farrar, what's the *matter* with you lately?" he said sharply.
>
> The younger man started, "Why . . . why . . ." The brusqueness of the other's manner shocked him suddenly into confession. "I've lost my nerve, Professor Mallory, that's what's the matter with me. I'm frightened to death," he said melodramatically.
>
> "What *of*?" asked Mallory, with a little challenge in his tone.
>
> The flood-gates were open. The younger man burst out in exclamations, waving his thin, nervous, knotted fingers, his face twitching as he spoke, "Of myself . . . no, not myself, but my body! I'm not well . . . I'm getting worse all the time. The doctors don't make out what is the matter . . . I don't sleep . . . I worry . . . I forget things, I take no interest in life . . . the doctors intimate a nervous breakdown ahead of me . . . and yet I rest . . . I rest . . . more than I can afford to! I never go out. Every evening I'm in bed by nine o'clock. I take no part in college life beyond my work, for fear of the nervous strain. I've refused to take charge of that summer school in New York, you know, that would be such an opportunity for me . . . if I could only sleep! But though I never do anything exciting in the evening . . . heavens! What nights I have. Black hours of seeing myself in a sanitarium, dependent on my brother! I never . . . why, I'm in hell . . . that's what's the matter with me, a perfect hell of ignoble terror!"

Summary

Professor Mallory asks Farrar what is wrong with him. Farrar replies that he can't sleep, and he worries. He is afraid he is headed for a nervous breakdown, and will end up in a sanitarium, dependent on his brother.

Practice

Read another passage from "The Heyday of the Blood," and write a summary of it in the space given below.

> "You don't suppose those great friends of yours, the nerve specialists, would object to my telling you a story, do you? It's very quiet and unexciting. You're not too busy?"
>
> "Busy! I've forgotten the meaning of the word! I don't dare to be!"
>
> "Very well, then; I mean to carry you back to the stony little farm in the Green Mountains, where I had the extreme good luck to be born and raised. You've heard me speak of Hillsboro; and the story is all about my great-grandfather, who came to live with us when I was a little boy."
>
> "Your great-grandfather?" said the other incredulously. "People don't remember their great-grandfathers!"
>
> "Oh, yes, they do, in Vermont. There was my father on one farm, and my grandfather on another, without a thought that he was no longer young, and there was 'gran'ther' as we called him, eighty-eight years old and just persuaded to settle back, let his descendants take care of him, and consent to be an old man. He had been in the War of 1812—think of that, you mushroom!—and had lost an arm and a good deal of his health there. He had lately begun to get a pension of twelve dollars a month, so that for an old man he was quite independent financially, as poor Vermont farmers look at things; and he was a most extraordinary character, so that his arrival in our family was quite an event.

PARAPHRASE

Introduction

When effective readers **paraphrase**, they take an author's words and think them through using their previous knowledge and experience. Then they are ready to recreate the author's message using their own words.

Paraphrasing is a great way for you to check your understanding of a piece you've read. If you can restate information correctly and communicate it to others then you most likely have mastered it. Follow these tips when you paraphrase.

- As you read, ask yourself what the author is saying.
- Think of other ways you could say the same thing.
- Look up any words you are not familiar with.

Model

Read this portion of "Paul Revere's Ride," by Henry Wadsworth Longfellow. Then study the paraphrased sample given below. Notice that while the writer of the paraphrased version uses different language, exactly the same information is presented. All essential details are included. The paraphrased version also includes new information—the exact year— which is placed in parentheses to separate it from the paraphrased work.

> Listen, my children, and you shall hear
> Of the midnight ride of Paul Revere.
> On the eighteenth of April in Seventy-five;
> Hardly a man is now alive
> Who remembers that famous day and year.
>
> He said to his friend, "If the British march
> By land or sea from the town to-night,
> Hang a lantern aloft in the belfry arch
> Of the North Church tower as a signal light,—
> One, if by land, and two, if by sea;
> And I on the opposite shore will be,
> Ready to ride and spread the alarm
> Through every Middlesex village and farm,
> For the country folk to be up and to arm."
>
> Then he said, "Good night!" and with muffled oar
> Silently rowed to the Charlestown shore . . .

Paraphrase

The narrator of the poem is telling the story of Paul Revere's midnight ride on April 18, '75 (we know it was 1775, because it was during the American Revolution). Revere told his friend to let him know if the British were marching on them that night by hanging one lantern in the church belfry if they were coming by land, and two if they were coming by sea. Revere would watch from the opposite shore and then ride on his horse to spread the alarm throughout Middlesex. Then Revere told his friend good night, and rowed away silently to the Charlestown shore.

Practice

Read another passage from Longfellow's poem, then paraphrase what you have read in the space provided below.

> Meanwhile, impatient to mount and ride,
> Booted and spurred, with a heavy stride
> On the opposite shore walked Paul Revere.
> Now he patted his horse's side,
> Now gazed at the landscape far and near,
> Then, impetuous, stamped the earth.
> And turned and tightened his saddle-girth;
> But mostly he watched with eager search
> The belfry-tower of the Old North Church,
> As it rose above the graves on the hill,
> Lonely and spectral and somber and still.
> And lo! As he looks, on the belfry's height
> A glimmer, and then a gleam of light!
> He springs to the saddle, the bridle he turns,
> But lingers and gazes till full on his sight
> A second lamp in the belfry burns!

____

____

____

____

____

____

____

____

____

FORM GENERALIZATIONS

Introduction

Authors often give readers specific clues which fit together like a puzzle, enabling readers to gain a broader, basic understanding of the reading material. The process of going from specific clues to broader understanding is **forming generalizations.**

To form generalizations when you are reading, remember that you must:
- Read through the passage.
- Search for clues in the text. Look for words or actions that are repeated, or connect to each other in some way.
- Decide how those clues fit together. Is there a larger meaning when the clues are put together than when each is examined separately? Can you make an assumption about the story that was not clear before?

If so, you have formed a generalization.

Model

Read this excerpt from the play, "Let Me Hear You Whisper," by Paul Zindel. Can you form any generalizations from this passage? See if your ideas agree with the examples given below.

> Miss Moray. Helen, why don't you dust for a while? Vary your labors. *[She swings open a shelf area to reveal rather hideously preserved specimens. Helen looks ready to gag as she sees the jars of all sizes. Various animals and parts of animals are visible in their formaldehyde baths.]* A feather duster— here—is marvelous for dusting though a damp rag may be necessary for the glass surfaces. But whatever—do be careful. Margaurita once dropped a jar of assorted North Atlantic eels.
>
> *[Miss Moray smiles and exits in the elevator, leaving Helen alone. She is most uncomfortable in the environment . . .]*

Generalization
This is not Helen's favorite place to work.
This sentence expresses a broad understanding of the excerpt.

Clues from the text
Helen looks ready to gag when she sees the jars of preserved animals.
When Miss Moray leaves Helen alone, she is most uncomfortable in the environment.
This sentence gives clues in order to form the generalization.

Practice

Read an excerpt from another scene of "Let Me Hear You Whisper," and answer the questions that follow.

HELEN pushes her equipment into the lab. The curtain on the DOLPHIN's tank has been closed. She sets her items up, then goes to the tank and pulls the curtain open a moment. The DOLPHIN is looking at her. She closes the curtain and starts scrubbing. The thought of the DOLPHIN amuses her a moment, relieving the tension she feels about the mamma . . . She opens the curtain so she can watch the DOLPHIN as she works. She and the DOLPHIN stare at each other and HELEN appears to be more curious than worried . . . She goes to the DOLPHIN's tank and notices how sad it looks . . . She bends down and looks directly into the DOLPHIN's face. He lets out a bubble at her. She sticks her tongue out at him. She makes an exaggerated smile, and is very curious about what his skin feels like. She reaches her hand in and just touches the top of his head. He squirms and likes it, but she's interested in drying off her finger. She returns to scrubbing for a minute, then can't resist more fully petting the DOLPHIN. This time he reacts even more enthusiastically. She is half afraid and half happy.

1. What generalization(s) can you form from this passage?

____

____

____

____

2. What clues from the text did you use in forming your generalization(s)?

____

____

____

____

NAME _______________________________   DATE __________

MAKE JUDGMENTS

Introduction

Effective readers are called upon to read critically, which includes forming their own opinions of the characters and their actions. This is called **making judgments**. When you are reading, gather evidence from the information given by the author, and make judgments based on that information. Remember that the judgments you make are also based on your previous knowledge and experience. Therefore, judgments or opinions are subjective—they can vary widely from one reader to another. Keep in mind not to make a judgment before all the evidence is given.

Model

Read the following passage from "The Old Grandfather and His Little Grandson," by Leo Tolstoy. Can you make any judgments of the characters and their actions from the information found here? See if your ideas agree with those given below.

> The grandfather had become very old. His legs would not carry him, his eyes could not see, his ears could not hear, and he was toothless. When he ate, bits of food sometimes dropped out of his mouth. His son and his son's wife no longer allowed him to eat with them at the table. He had to eat his meals in the corner near the stove.
>
> One day they gave him his food in a bowl. He tried to move the bowl closer; it fell to the floor and broke. His daughter-in-law scolded him. She told him that he spoiled everything in the house and broke their dishes, and she said that from now on he would get his food in a wooden dish. The old man sighed and said nothing.

Judgments

- The grandfather could not help his condition—it was due to old age.

It is relatively easy to make a judgment about the grandfather. The son and daughter-in-law, however, are a little trickier.

- The grandfather's son and daughter-in-law treated him very unkindly.

This statement is accurate, based on the information in the passage above. But can the reader make a blanket judgment that the son and daughter-in-law are not well-meaning people? What do you think?

Practice

Read the rest of the story, "The Old Grandfather and His Little Grandson," and answer the questions that follow.

A few days later, the old man's son and his wife were sitting in their hut, resting and watching their little boy playing on the floor. They saw him putting together something out of small pieces of wood. His father asked him, "What are you making, Misha?"

The little grandson said, "I'm making a wooden bucket. When you and Mamma get old, I'll feed you out of this wooden dish."

The young peasant and his wife looked at each other, and tears filled their eyes. They were ashamed because they had treated the old grandfather so meanly, and from that day they again let the old man eat with them at the table and took better care of him.

1. Has your judgment about the old grandfather's son and daughter-in-law changed? Why or why not?

____

____

____

____

2. What about the little grandson? Is he playing innocently, or is he trying to teach his parents a lesson?

____

____

____

____

3. What are your thoughts about the grandfather?

____

____

____

____

NAME ____ **DATE** __________

Read the following passage. Then answer the questions that follow. Write the letter of the correct answer on the line at the right.

> The moon, like to a silver bow
>   new-bent in heaven.
>   William Shakespeare

1. What two things are compared?   1. ______
   A. the moon and heaven
   B. a silver bow and heaven
   C. the moon and a silver bow
   D. none of the above

2. Which of the following best describes this moon?   2. ______
   A. new moon
   B. full moon
   C. quarter moon
   D. half moon

3. Read the sentence. Then choose the meaning of the underlined word. Write   3. ______
   the letter of the answer on the line at the right.

> Nowhere, wrote T. S. Eliot, was there a cat as <u>deceitful</u> as Macavity, the "Hidden Paw."

   A. arrogant
   B. lazy
   C. dishonest
   D. beautiful

4. Read the sentence. Then choose the meaning of the underlined word. Write   4. ______
   the letter of the answer on the line at the right.

> In "A Dream Deferred," Langston Hughes examines the <u>disastrous</u> effects of frustrated hopes.

   A. common   **C.** causing suffering
   B. permanent   **D.** unending

Read the following passage. Then answer the question that follows. Write the letter of the correct answer on the line at the right.

> I was always late for class. We had a piano lesson before the dancing lesson and the traveling between required at least forty minutes and getting into practice clothes another ten. Mother allowed twenty minutes exactly from the keyboard to barre and in three years she refused to adjust her timetable, always hoping that geography would somehow give way. As a consequence I always missed the preliminary warming-up exercises and started every class half through, cold and unprepared. I was not permitted ever to make the trip into town alone so I could not better the situation. Mother gave up two afternoons a week, a noteworthy sacrifice in a busy life, to driving us downtown. She never put off one class in three years, but she also was never on time.

NAME _______________________________________ DATE _____________

5. Which of the following statements is supported by the information given in
   the passage?
   A. The narrator's mother did not approve of her daughter's dancing lessons.
   B. Children are unable to juggle a crowded after-school schedule.
   C. It is unwise for one person to study both dance and piano.
   D. The narrator's mother was stubborn, strict, and unbending in her ways.

5. _______

Read the following passage. Then answer the questions that follow. Write the letter
of the correct answer on the line at the right.

> Where did the idea of a park come from? In the early 1800s New York was already
> a "tumultuous and brutal city," packed into the lower part of the island of
> Manhattan. Businessmen were bent on buying up and making a profit from
> every square foot of the city's tight space. If this kept on, some feared, masses
> of New Yorkers would be crowded to death. It was a few thoughtful people, led
> by the poet and newspaper editor William Cullen Bryant and the writer
> Washington Irving, who imagined what a great open space could do to bring light
> and air and peace and quiet to the harried souls of the great city. And especially
> to the children.

6. Which of the following statements best expresses the author's strong feelings
   about New York?
   A. The author considers the city noisy and violent, the businessmen money
      hungry, and the population explosive and tormented.
   B. The author regards the city as busy, exciting, and full of energetic, goal-
      oriented people.
   C. The author believes the city is a great place for adults and children.
   D. The author despises New York and concludes that the only answer is to
      move to a quiet, peaceful part of the country.

6. _______

7. Which of the following remarks would this author be most likely to voice to a
   New York businessman of the 1800s?
   A. "You have my complete support in your industrial endeavors."
   B. "If this city turns into one colossal garbage basket chock-full of people and
      debris, you will be among the first people each citizen blames."
   C. "New York would not be one of the most popular cities in the world without
      men such as you."
   D. "Can you imagine how uninteresting, quiet, and backward Manhattan was
      before clever people such as you bought it from the Indians?"

7. _______

<table>
<tr><td>NAME</td><td>DATE</td></tr>
</table>

Read the following passage. Then answer the questions that follow. Write the letter of the correct answer on the line at the right.

> I looked up from my typewriter one late afternoon, a little startled. A boy stood at the door, and my pointer dog, my companion, was at his side and had not barked to warn me. The boy was probably twelve years old, but undersized. He wore overalls and a torn shirt, and was barefooted.
>
> He said, "I can chop some wood today."
>
> I said, "But I have a boy coming from the orphanage."
>
> "I'm the boy."
>
> "You? But you're so small."
>
> "Size don't matter, chopping wood," he said. "Some of the big boys don't chop good. I've been chopping wood at the orphanage a long time."
>
> I visualized mangled and inadequate branches for my fires. I was well into my work and not inclined to conversation. I was a little blunt.
>
> "Very well. There's the ax. Go ahead and see what you can do."

8. Which of the following is an opinion presented in the selection?   8. _____
   A. The boy was unenthusiastic about working for the narrator.
   B. The boy was small for his age.
   C. The narrator generally distrusted other people.
   D. The narrator doubted the boy's ability to do the work.

9. Which of the following is a fact presented in the selection?   9. _____
   A. The narrator's dog was a pointer.
   B. The boy's attire was insufficient and unattractive.
   C. Size was not related to the boy's ability to chop wood.
   D. The narrator was a mystery writer.

Read the following passage. Then answer the questions that follow. Write the letter of the correct answer on the line at the right.

> The latest blight to afflict the spoken word in the United States is the rapidly spreading reiteration of the phrase, "you know." I don't know just when it began moving like a rainstorm through the language, but I tremble at its increasing garbling of meaning, ruining of rhythm, and drumming upon my hapless ears. One man, in a phone conversation with me last summer, used the phrase thirty-four times in about five minutes, by my own count; a young matron in Chicago got seven "you knows" into one wavy sentence, and I have also heard it as far west as Denver, where an otherwise charming woman at a garden party in August said it almost as often as a whippoorwill says, "Whippoorwill." Once, speaking of whippoorwills, I was waked after midnight by one of those feathered hellions and lay there counting his chants. He got up to one hundred and fifty-eight and then suddenly said, "Whip—" and stopped dead. I like to believe that his mate, at the end of her patience, finally let him have it.

10. Which statement best expresses the main idea of the passage? 10. ______
    A. A disturbing new trend is threatening English conversation.
    B. Throughout the United States, people use the same informal expressions.
    C. Doubting his own sanity, the author has mistaken bird calls for human conversation.
    D. Unlike people, whippoorwills never interrupt their cry.

11. How far to the west did the author find evidence of the phenomenon 11. ______
    he described?
    A. Chicago
    B. the Rocky Mountains
    C. Denver
    D. Seattle

12. Which of the following meanings of *garble* apply to its use in the selection? 12. ______
    A. to select the best parts of
    B. to confuse or mix up (a quotation, story, message, etc.) unintentionally
    C. to suppress or distort parts of (a story, etc.) in telling, so as to mislead
       or misrepresent

13. Using context clues in the passage, choose the meaning of *hellion*. 13. ______
    A. troublemaker
    B. creature
    C. beauty
    D. bird

14. What is the author's purpose in writing about the widespread use of the phrase, 14. ______
    "you know"?
    A. The author wants to inform people of speech habits in various parts of the
       United States.
    B. The author wants to persuade people to speak intelligently and correctly,
       unlike birds that repeat sounds ceaselessly.
    C. The author wants to entertain readers with his or her descriptions of human
       and bird communication habits.
    D. The author wants to express his or her negative opinion of the habit of
       using the phrase, "you know," as well as make fun of people who use it.

15. Which of the following statements best describes the author's point of view 15. ______
    toward the use of the phrase, "you know"?
    A. The author is in favor of repetitious speech patterns.
    B. The author opposes speech habits that interfere with the natural flow
       of conversation.
    C. The author stands against speech habits that influence the entire United States.
    D. The author is in favor of improved environmental conditions to preserve
       the whippoorwill.

NAME ___________________________________ **DATE** __________

Use this map to answer the following questions.

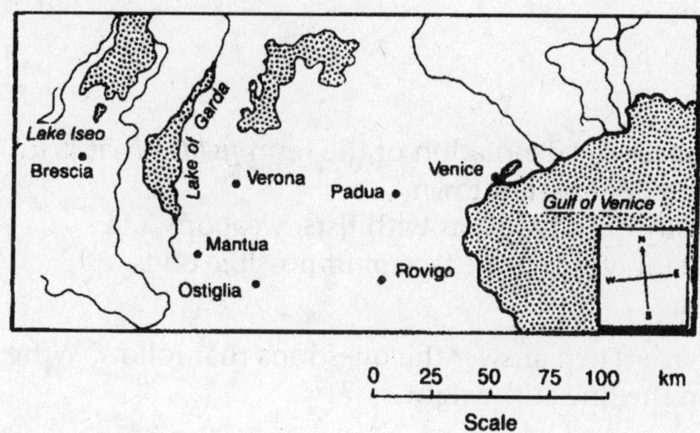

16. What city is closest to Mantua?   16. ______
    A. Rovigo
    B. Verona
    C. Ostiglia
    D. Venice

17. What is the largest body of water shown on the map?   17. ______
    A. the Gulf of Venice
    B. The Lake of Garda
    C. the Mediterranean Sea
    D. Lake Iseo

Read the following passage. Then answer the questions that follow. Write the letter of the correct answer on the line at the right.

"Don't you come in here," my mother warned me.

I froze in my tracks and stared at her.

"But they're coming after me," I said.

"You just stay right where you are," she said in a deadly tone. "I'm going to teach you this night to stand up and fight for yourself."

She went into the house and I waited, terrified, wondering what she was about. Presently she returned with more money and another note; she also had a long, heavy stick.

"Take this money, this note, and this stick," she said. "Go to the store and buy those groceries. If those boys bother you, then fight." . . .

. . . They closed in. In blind fear I let the stick fly, feeling it crack against a boy's skull . . . .

. . . That night, I won the right to the streets of Memphis.

18. What can you generalize about how a person survives in this boy's neighborhood?   18. ______
    A. by staying at home and not venturing onto the streets
    B. by staying in groups
    C. by having money
    D. by fighting for one's freedom to walk the streets safely

                                     Post-Test **79**

19. What would the mother's connotation of the term *fight* be?　　　　19. ______
    A. defeat
    B. survival
    C. battle
    D. struggle

20. The narrator experiences the denotation of the term *fight*. What is it?　　20. ______
    A. to survive in a turbulent part of town
    B. to oppose physically or in battle, as with fists, weapons, etc.
    C. to put forth a gallant effort in the face of impossible odds
    D. to stand up to fear

Read the following passage. Then answer the questions that follow. Write the letter of the correct answer on the line at the right.

> Ah but there was a glory in that room! Each day's class was important and a little frightening. When the master praised a pupil we shivered with envy and excitement. When he roared and denounced we blanched. When he made jokes we laughed although we rarely understood what he was saying—it nearly always had to do with teasing some wretch. When he talked about expression and "sowl" I, for one, wept. When he talked about fame, galas, "applows," and *réclame*,[1] I slept poorly for nights after. We curtsied formally at the end of the class. We were never late—that is, the others were never late, I always was. When he talked of his triumphs with Diaghilev[2] in Paris, and how the pupils practice in Moscow with butter on the floor to make it harder, and how as a young man he could easily turn twenty pirouettes[3] with a single push, we listened round-eyed, grabbing the chance to get our breaths before the next frantic series of jumps.

1. *réclame* (rā kläm'): French for "publicity."
2. **Diaghilev:** Sergei Pavlovich Diaghilev (syer gya'i päv o vich dyä' gi lyef), famous Russian ballet producer (1872–1929).
3. **pirouettes** (pir oo wetz) *n.*: Rapid turns on one foot or the point of the toe.

21. What was done in Moscow to make it harder for ballet students to dance?　　21. ______
    A. They were kept up late.
    B. Butter was spread on the floor.
    C. Instructions were given in French.
    D. Teachers never allowed students to get their breath.

22. Which of the following differences between the narrator and the master is the　22. ______
    most likely to be true?
    A. The narrator weeps at the master's description of expression; the master
       probably never wept as a student.
    B. The narrator gets tired between series of jumps; the master, as a student,
       most likely never grew tired at his practices.
    C. The narrator is always late; the master, as a student, was most likely never late.
    D. The narrator misses sleep when he or she ponders fame; the master probably
       never considered the possibility of becoming famous.

Read the following passage. Then answer the questions that follow. Write the letter of the correct answer on the line at the right.

> There was a loud rumbling sound; the cave darkened. Ulysses whirled around. He saw that the door had been closed. The far end of the cavern was too dark to see anything, but then—amazed, aghast—he saw what looked like a huge red lantern far above, coming closer. Then he saw the great shadow of a nose under it, and the gleam of teeth. He realized that the lantern was a great flaming eye. Then he saw the whole giant, tall as a tree, with huge fingers reaching out of the shadows, fingers bigger than baling hooks. They closed around two sailors and hauled them screaming into the air.

23. Which of the following statements best summarizes the creature's appearance?　　**23.** _______
   A. The creature, tall as a tree, has a great flaming eye, a huge nose, gleaming teeth, and huge fingers.
   B. The creature lives in an unlit cave and closes the door to capture intruders.
   C. The creature uses his huge fingers to haul two sailors into the air.
   D. Ulysses is amazed at the towering, ghastly figure.

24. What conclusion can you draw about the two sailors' fate?　　**24.** _______
   A. They are going to become the huge creature's pets.
   B. They are going to be rescued by Ulysses.
   C. They are going to die.
   D. They are going to have to battle the monster.

25. What is Ulysses's first clue that he and his men have stumbled into dangerous territory?　　**25.** _______
   A. Ulysses notices what appears to be a huge red lantern hanging far above him and moving in his direction.
   B. Ulysses beholds the entire figure of a huge one-eyed monster.
   C. Ulysses sees the creature grab two sailors.
   D. Ulysses realizes that the cave's door has been closed.

26. Where would you most likely find information to help you determine what a baling hook is?　　**26.** _______
   A. almanac
   B. thesaurus
   C. encyclopedia
   D. dictionary

Read the following passage. Then answer the questions that follow. Write the letter of the correct answer on the line at the right.

"And I . . . I suppose you'll want me to get that can off him."

"Oh, yes, yes, please!"

It took all my strength to lift him onto the table. He was heavier now than before his illness. I reached for the familiar forceps and began to turn the jagged edges of the can outwards from the nose and mouth. Tomato soup must have been one of his favorites because he was really deeply embedded, and it took some time before I was able to slide the can from his face.

I fought off his slobbering attack. "He's back in the dustbins, I see."

"Yes, he is quite regularly. I've pulled several cans off him myself. And he goes sliding with the children, too." She smiled happily.

Thoughtfully I took my stethoscope from the pocket of my white coat and listened to his lungs. They were wonderfully clear . . .

. . . "But Mr. Herriot," Mrs. Westby's eyes were wide, "how on earth has this happened? How has he got better?"

. . . "The healing power of nature. Something no veterinary surgeon can compete with when it decides to act."

"I see. And you can never tell when this is going to happen?"

"No."

27. Which statement best expresses the implied main idea of the passage?   27. _______
   A. The dog's tomato soup can episodes demonstrate his return to health.
   B. Using forceps is the only way to remove a tomato soup can from a dog's nose and mouth.
   C. Tomato is the dog's favorite flavor of soup.
   D. If a dog regularly eats tomato soup, he will not suffer from lung ailments.

28. Select the statement below that best supports the main idea of the selection.   28. _______
   A. The dog slobbers when he "attacks" Mr. Herriot.
   B. Mr. Herriot puts the dog on a table before he examines him.
   C. Mr. Herriot uses forceps to loosen the can from the dog's nose and mouth.
   D. Mrs. Westby has pulled several tomato soup cans off the dog's nose and mouth.

29. Which of the following statements best supports Mr. Herriot's assertion that no   29. _______
   surgeon can compete with the healing power of nature?
   A. Natural healing only occurs in association with a veterinary surgeon's actions.
   B. When an animal does not recover from an injury or illness, it is always due to the veterinarian's incompetence.
   C. A veterinary surgeon is limited in what he or she can do for a sick animal, but nature can heal any ailment when it chooses to do so.
   D. An animal's recovery is totally dependent on a veterinarian's skills, tools, and medicines.

Read the following passage. Then answer the questions that follow. Write the letter of the correct answer on the line at the right.

> The priest walked toward the kitchen, and Leon stood with his cap in his hand, playing with the earflaps and examining the living room—the brown sofa, the green armchair, and the brass lamp that hung down from the ceiling by links of chain. The priest dragged a chair out of the kitchen and offered it to Leon.
>
> "No thank you, Father. I only came to ask you if you would bring your holy water to the graveyard."
>
> The priest turned away from Leon and looked out the window at the patio full of shadows and the dining-room windows of the nuns' cloister across the patio. The curtains were heavy, and the light from within faintly penetrated; it was impossible to see the nuns inside eating supper. "Why didn't you tell me he was dead? I could have brought the Last Rites[1] anyway."

1. the Last Rites: A religious ceremony for a dying person or someone who has just died.

30. What did the priest do after Leon asked him to come to the graveyard?　　30. ______
    A. He brought Leon a chair from the kitchen.
    B. He watched the nuns eating their supper.
    C. He drove to the graveyard to console Leon's family.
    D. He turned from Leon and looked out the window.

31. Which of the following can be concluded from this passage?　　31. ______
    A. Leon's relationship with the priest was relaxed and friendly.
    B. The priest was disturbed by Leon's request.
    C. Holy water was scarce and was seldom sprinkled on graves.
    D. The priest was dismayed by the large number of recent deaths.

32. Nuns and priests devote their lives to service and prayer to God; therefore the　　32. ______
    connotation of the word *cloister*, which appears in the selection, would most
    likely be which of the following?
    A. retirement from the world
    B. a place of religious seclusion: monastery or convent
    C. monastic life
    D. an arched way or covered walk along the inside wall or walls of a monastery,
       convent, church, or college building

33. Which of the following words or groups of words is not a denotation of the　　33. ______
    word *cloister*?
    A. a convent
    B. a monastery
    C. any place where one may lead an isolated life
    D. the nuns' favorite place to be on Friday nights

Read the following passage. Then answer the questions that follow. Write the letter of the correct answer on the line at the right.

> I'm very tired of being a nice person, Miss Moray. I'm going to report you to the ASPCA,[1] or somebody, because . . . I've decided I don't like you cutting the heads off mice and sawing through skulls of St. Bernards . . . and if being a nice person is just not saying anything and letting you pack of butchers run around doing whatever you want, then I don't want to be nice anymore. (*Pause*) You gotta be very stupid people to need an animal to talk before you know just from looking at it that it's saying something . . . that it knows what pain feels like. I'd like to see you all with a few electrodes in your heads. Being nice isn't any good. (*Looking at* DOLPHIN) They just kill you off if you do that. And that's being a coward. You gotta talk back. You gotta speak up against what's wrong and bad, or you can't ever stop it. At least you've gotta try. (*She bursts into tears.*)

1. **ASPCA:** American Society for the Prevention of Cruelty to Animals.

34. Which of the following statements best expresses the problem the speaker is addressing?
    A. Remaining quiet about a bad situation such as animal abuse will not abolish it.
    B. Cutting the heads off mice is a disgusting practice.
    C. Animals know what pain feels like.
    D. People and animals are killed when they are nice.

34. ______

35. What is the speaker's solution to the problem?
    A. to put electrodes in the humans' heads
    B. to become a coward and remain quiet
    C. to kidnap the mice and St. Bernards before they are destroyed
    D. to speak up against what is wrong and bad

35. ______

Read the following passage. Then answer the questions that follow. Write the letter of the correct answer on the line at the right.

> She reached Lewes late on Tuesday night. In those days, I must tell you, there was no bridge over the river at Southease, nor had the road to Newhaven yet been made. To reach Rodmell it was necessary to cross the river Ouse by a ford, traces of which still exist, but this could only be attempted at low tide, when the stones on the river bed appeared above the water. Mr. Stacey, the farmer, was going to Rodmell in his cart, and he kindly offered to take Mrs. Gage with him.

36. What is the relationship between low tide and Mr. Stacey's ability to drive his cart across the river Ouse?
    A. At low tide, the Ouse's waters are at a high point, and Mr. Stacey's cart will float from one side of the river to the other.
    B. At low tide, rocks stick out of the water and make the trip across the river bumpy and uncomfortable.
    C. At low tide, the river is shallow, and Mr. Stacey can drive his cart across.
    D. At low tide, the horses pulling Mr. Stacey's cart are less afraid to cross the river.

36. ______

NAME _______________________________________   **DATE** ____________

37. What causes Mr. Stacey and Mrs. Gage to have to cross the river Ouse to get to Rodmell?   37. ______
   A. The stones on the river bed are appearing above the water.
   B. Mr. Stacey is a farmer who must get to Rodmell.
   C. There is no bridge over the river at Southease, nor has the road to Newhaven been constructed.
   D. Mr. Stacey is kind and offers to take Mrs. Gage to Rodmell.

38. Use the context clues in the selection to choose the definition of the term *ford*.   38. ______
   A. a shallow place in a stream, river, etc., where one can cross
   B. an automobile produced in the United States
   C. situated in front of some other thing or part
   D. a narrow inlet or arm of the sea bordered by steep cliffs

Read the following passage. Then answer the questions that follow. Write the letter of the correct answer on the line at the right.

> During the winter when I was twelve years old a gale of abnormal force swept the Great Lakes region. Gusts reached almost hurricane proportions. Weakened by the work of the fungus, bacteria, woodpeckers, and beetles, the whole top of the tree snapped off some seventy feet from the ground. After that the progress of its dissolution was rapid.
>
> Finally the last of the lower leaves disappeared. The green badge of life returned no more. On summer days the sound of the wind sweeping the old oak had a winter shrillness. No more was there the rustling of a multitude of leaves above our hammock; no more was there the "plump!" of falling acorns. Leaves and acorns, life and progress, were at an end.

39. Some information in the selection is important and some is unimportant. Choose the statement below that is not important to the main idea of this passage.   39. ______
   A. The tree was weakened by the work of the fungus, bacteria, woodpeckers, and beetles.
   B. The tree deteriorated rapidly after its top broke off.
   C. The narrator was twelve years old when the gale force wind snapped the treetop.
   D. Finally the tree stopped producing leaves.

40. According to this selection, what caused the top of the tree to break off?   40. ______
   A. A hurricane swept through the Great Lakes region.
   B. An unusually strong wind struck the already weakened tree.
   C. Bacteria, woodpeckers, and beetles attacked the upper branches of the tree.
   D. The tree was severely pruned by a construction crew.

41. Which of the following statements best reflects the author's attitude toward the death of the tree?   41. ______
   A. He regretfully accepted the absence of the tree from his life.
   B. He was relieved that its ugly decline was completed.
   C. He was angered by the waste of a beautiful, important symbol.
   D. He hopefully planted a young tree in place of the dead one.

42. Using context clues provided in the selection, choose the meaning of the
    term *dissolution*.
    A. decay
    B. repair
    C. toppling
    D. growth

42. ______

Read the following passage. Then answer the questions that follow. Write the letter
of the correct answer on the line at the right.

> Bennie got up from the edge of the porch and ran around the house. The two
> old women paid no attention to his going. He knew what his grandmother would
> say to Miss May. She would tell Miss May how she wanted to be dressed for
> burial. She would name the song she wanted to be sung over her. He had heard
> the same conversation many times. Now it was different. What they were talking
> about would soon "come to pass," as his grandmother would say. Miss May did
> not know, but he knew.

43. Which of the following statements is an opinion presented in the selection?
    A. Bennie was shocked to hear his grandmother discuss her burial plans.
    B. Bennie left the porch and went behind the house.
    C. Knowing of his grandmother's ill health, Bennie couldn't bear to listen to
       her conversation with Miss May.
    D. Bennie suspected that both his grandmother and Miss May would soon die.

43. ______

44. Which of the following statements is supported by the information given in
    the passage?
    A. Bennie was unfamiliar with the topic of death.
    B. Bennie was beginning to understand that his grandmother would soon die.
    C. People who dwell on death lead miserable lives.
    D. Young children are incapable of believing that people die.

44. ______

Read the sentence below and answer the question that follows. Write the letter of
the correct answer on the line at the right.

> Driving snow, a wind that cut like a white-hot knife, and darkness, had forced
> them to grope for a camping place.

45. Which of the following sentences paraphrases the sentence above?
    A. Snow, wind, and darkness forced them to look for a place to camp.
    B. Snow that cut like a white-hot knife forced them to look for a camping place.
    C. Driving snow, a wind that cut like a white-hot knife, and darkness had
       forced them to grope for a camping place.
    D. Darkness forced them out of the snowy woods.

45. ______